F W DE KLERK

F W DE KLERK

THE MAN IN HIS TIME

WILLEM DE KLERK

Jonathan Ball Publishers
Johannesburg

© Willem de Klerk, 1991

First published in 1991 by
Jonathan Ball Publishers
P O Box 2105
Parklands 2121
(011) 880-3116/7/8

ISBN 0 947464 36 0

PHOTOGRAPHIC ACKNOWLEDGEMENTS
Our sincere thanks to Marike de Klerk for allowing us access to the family
album for photographs of F W's early years.
The photograph of F W's visit to the Nancefield Hostel in Soweto by courtesy
of Robert Botha of *Business Day*.
All other photographs were kindly donated by the Bureau for Information,
Pretoria.

Translated by Henri Snijders

Typesetting and reproduction by Book Productions, Pretoria
Cover design by Michael Barnett
Front cover photograph by courtesy of the Bureau for Information, Pretoria
Back cover photograph by courtesy of *The Star*, Johannesburg
Printed and bound by National Book Printers, Goodwood, Cape

CONTENTS

FOREWORD

Who is F W de Klerk, and how has he changed the face of South African politics?

As his older brother, I will venture an answer to that question. It is most unusual for one brother to write about the other – it might even be construed as suspect. The plus is that I know him intimately. He has been before my eyes throughout his life, in a relationship that has always been candidly open. The minus is that the closeness of kinship might have clouded objectivity. For this I make no apology, because as far as involvement (common to every author and his subject) is concerned, this book is written with a measure of detachment: for years I have been a political commentator, striving for impartiality, truth and objectivity.

It was not my intention to write a biography or a comprehensive historical document. This is a factual portrait with the aid of the observations, knowledge and experience accumulated by myself and other people close to him; it is a commentary on South African politics with a particular accent on F W de Klerk's involvement. I have bound everything I have to say together with F W's political history rather than private family interactions.

Politics is very volatile in this country, and by the time this book appears there may well have been changes. I will try to give a synopsis of a few crucial events, with F W as chief actor: comprehensiveness is not the goal, but rather to illustrate the driving forces of South African politics and F W's life. The book is a marriage of the man and his time.

This aims to be an honest book, but it remains an interpretation and is therefore subjective. The man who is written about can in no way be held responsible for the author's opinions and conclusions.

1

THE STEEP STAIRS

1

On February 2, 1990, Frederik Willem de Klerk took the national salute from the lowest step outside the South African
Houses of Parliament. For him, as for his predecessors, this was
a special occasion: traditionally, the State President's opening
address to Parliament is a test of leadership and vision, a
message to the country and the world that the government of the
day has an intelligent grasp of its task and of the prerequisites
for peace, prosperity, and the well-being of its people. It is an
address in which the lines of government policy are clearly defined.

De Klerk knew that this was to be his acid test. Four and a half
months earlier, on September 20, 1989, he had been sworn in as
State President; now, for the first time, he would stand up
before a critical audience of despondent South Africans and a
cynical outside world.

On this day there was none of the pomp and circumstance that
marked most openings of Parliament under his predecessor,
P W Botha. Now there was no display of power by platoons of
soldiers, no march-pasts and aerial salutes; a solitary band
played the national anthem for the salute, and the customary
President's Guard was in attendance. The modesty of the
ceremony was in itself indicative of the soberness, humility and
calm that mark F W de Klerk's demeanour. As he himself put
it, 'It had to be a formal opening of Parliament, as is customary,

but at my request it was scaled down drastically. It had been done before. I do not like fanfares. This is my style, and to this I had kept since I was sworn in – an informal style that cuts down on ceremony as far as possible, without detracting from established traditions.'

Without further ceremony he mounted the steps to the chamber for joint sittings, where he was to open the Second Session of the Ninth Parliament of the Republic of South Africa. He knew what he was going to say, and why he wanted to say it.

What were his feelings in those moments? He summed them up with great certainty: 'In my own mind I had no doubts, because I was convinced that we were doing the right thing. I was about to say what was right. But I was a bit tenser than usual, because I realized that the implications were enormous, and that South Africa would never again be the same after that address.'

2

The text then waiting on the rostrum and the words in F W de Klerk's mind must be seen in the context of the many opening addresses the National Party had delivered to Parliament over the years.

Newspaper cuttings record a history of action and reaction, of intervention and pitfalls, of the deadly traps set by our political system. In those reports, human suffering – of blacks, of the victims of bomb explosions, of policemen – is given names and faces. Parliamentary opening addresses, on the other hand, are supposed to be a display of cold rationality, clinical policy statements, reports to the nation on the past, and prognoses for the future.

In that single address on February 2, 1990, F W de Klerk had to assimilate and supplement 41 years of opening addresses, deleting lines and scrapping paragraphs. His presidential address, as he himself put it in an interview, was designed to break through the barriers created by years of other opening addresses.

To me, those opening addresses revealed growing alienation on two fronts, both from the outside world and among South Africans at home. The address of February 2, 1990, was aimed at halting both forms of alienation.

As long ago as 1949, the Nationalist government had stated at the opening of Parliament that 'co-operation with the United Nations has been made difficult over the past three years by misunderstanding on issues vitally affecting the Union (*Hansard*, January 21, 1949). The next year it was reported that cordial relations between the Union and other members of the Commonwealth were being maintained (*Hansard*, January 20, 1950), and in 1951 that regular official visits at ministerial level were still promoting relations with other members of the Commonwealth and with the nations of Western Europe and the American continent (*Hansard*, January 19, 1951).

Worsening international relations were reflected in the words of 1952's opening address:

To their regret, however, my Ministers must state that owing to the serious infringement of South Africa's rights, and interference in her domestic affairs, by the United Nations Organization, they have been compelled to enter a strong protest including, *inter alia*, our withdrawal, at least for the present, from further participation in certain proceedings of that body.

(*Hansard*, January 18, 1952.)

In consequence, South Africa's delegation withdrew temporarily from the 1955 UNO session. In 1957, it was reported to Parliament that the government had decided to maintain only nominal representation at UNO (*Hansard*, January 18, 1957).

The 1961 presidential address by South Africa's first State President, C R Swart, sounded the alarm on our relations with Western countries:

Faced as we are with unique problems, South Africa's traditional relations with other Western States are being subjected to strains which only time and patience can relieve. My Government is confident that our friendships, rooted in history, will survive the impact of the misunderstandings and suspicions which at present cloud our relations. To this end, my Government will persevere in its efforts to give visible proof of the true values which underlie its approach to South Africa's problems.

(*Hansard*, June 5, 1961.)

At the 1962 opening of Parliament, 'hostile blocs of nations and the aggressive attitude of the new African member-states' were mentioned. It was alleged that the communists were feeding the flames against us and that Western countries were trying 'to win the favour of the Afro-Asian states, even at the expense of sacrificing old friends and allies' (*Hansard*, January 19, 1962).

In the 1963 opening address, UNO sanctions and the formation of other fronts against us in Africa were seen as an onslaught on South African whites, founded on a distorted notion of our apartheid policy (*Hansard*, January 18, 1963).

And so the opening addresses continued: the unbridled vendettas against South Africa and the distorted impressions created by the world press (*Hansard*, January 17, 1964); the misrepresentation of South African legislation (*Hansard*, January 21, 1966); 'Anti-South African activities abroad are acquiring greater sophistication and financial support. Use is also being made of international pressures, which are directed not only against Western countries co-operating with South Africa, but particularly against countries in Africa, thus inhibiting the full and open development of inter-governmental relations with more African states' (*Hansard*, February 1, 1974).

In 1978 the State President's opening address to Parliament referred to the arms embargo and deplored the fact that the West was 'making common cause with radicals' against South Africa: 'The Republic of South Africa continues to be the target of a total onslaught being made on it on the political, economic, psychological, security and other fronts in an attempt to force it to abandon its present system of government.' (*Hansard*, January 27, 1978.)

The opening addresses of the eighties reflect puzzlement and incomprehension at the West's failure to respond more positively to all the government's reform measures and plans. It was stated repeatedly that domestic reforms were not designed merely to placate the outside world, but that foreign perceptions had to be taken into account:

In taking decisions in the interest of our country the Government must have regard to the fact that circumstances and events in the rest of the world have a definite influence on our country and our subcontinent. It is our responsibility

4

to take cognizance of the implications of the views of both friendly and hostile countries, and to take into account the effect of our decisions on the RSA's foreign relations. Indeed, our goal is to extend these relations; the interests of South Africa demand no less.

(Hansard, January 25, 1985.)

Complaints about South Africa's international dilemma came to a head in the State President's opening addresses between 1986 and 1989:

Yet, the campaign against the Republic of South Africa from abroad has greatly intensified.

On the one hand it has taken the form of an increased armed threat. This is proven by, among other things, the stock-piling of advanced armaments in certain neighbouring states and terror attacks across our borders. On the other hand, there were intensified attempts to isolate us in all spheres.

There are various reasons for this campaign. One is the fact that evolutionary reform does not serve the designs of leftist revolutionaries. The campaign is sustained by calculated lies about the South African realities which have, with doubtful motives, been spread across the world for so many decades. Attempts are continually being made to belittle each step forward and to brand all Government initiatives as merely cosmetic, while conditions more appalling than those ostensibly prevailing in South Africa are sanctimoniously tolerated elsewhere in the world.

(Hansard, January 31, 1986.)

In 1986, our international position was characterised increasingly by intensified pressures and punitive actions against our country. Undisguised attempts at interference in our domestic affairs reached unprecedented proportions.

This sad reflection on the conscience of a troubled world is both disturbing and ironical – especially since it came about while we were proceeding apace with our programme of reform and renewal and had made significant progress in removing discrimination. *(Hansard*, January 30, 1987.)

Amid these positive developments, there are indications that elements in the international community are still intent on intensifying the vindictive sanctions campaign against South Africa, despite the obvious damaging effect for all the countries of the region. *(Hansard*, February 3, 1989.)

Of his opening address on February 2, 1990, F W de Klerk said, 'That speech was mainly aimed at breaking our stalemate in Africa and the West. Internationally we were teetering on the edge of the abyss.'

Opening addresses since 1949 do indeed provide a window on South Africa's international isolation. At the same time, they reveal yet another cancerous growth that F W de Klerk had to try to excise on February 2, 1990: internal revolt against apartheid.

At the opening of Parliament in 1949, the concept of a total onslaught against South Africa, and efforts to fend it off, were put in a nutshell:

My Ministers are, after investigation, gravely concerned at the considerable dimensions already assumed by Communistic activities amongst certain classes of the population and are at present considering the necessary steps to combat them effectively.

My Ministers intend to take the necessary steps, by means of legislative as well as administrative measures, to give effect to their policy of segregation and rendering permanent better relations between the European and non-European races, on a sound and just basis.

(*Hansard*, January 21, 1949.)

In the next three opening addresses it was announced that 'the flow of native labour to farms and to cities would be channelled effectively' (*Hansard*, January 20, 1950); that the production capacity of the homelands would be increased (*Hansard*, January 20, 1950); that 'Natives will be encouraged to equip themselves for increased participation in and responsibility for their own services' (*Hansard*, January 19, 1951); and that legislation and administrative measures would be invoked 'to promote the healthy development of the Bantu population on the broad basis of self-expression within their own territory and within their own community' (*Hansard*, January 18, 1952).

In fact, each opening address added yet another strand to a tapestry of apartheid legislation that would become, under Dr Verwoerd, a finespun mesh from which no black could hope to escape.

The first crack in the wall was reported in the 1953 opening address:

There have been several instances of Native riots and violence in the vicinity of some of the larger cities. A resistance campaign against laws of the country was initiated by certain Indian and Native leaders and organizations, and was

6

supported also by Europeans. The Government took the necessary steps to deal with this lawlessness and the resistance campaign is at present under control. The Government however finds it necessary to ask Parliament for certain additional powers which will enable it to deal swiftly and effectively with possible eventualities.

(*Hansard*, January 23, 1953.)

The first attempt at negotiation was announced in 1955:

Consultations with Bantu chiefs who were accompanied by counsellors from both Native areas and urban locations took place at special gatherings and this practice, which has the support of the Natives, will be further developed. The Government have noted with satisfaction the growing support among the Bantu of the policy of separate development.

(*Hansard*, January 21, 1955.)

In what was obviously a major policy statement, the entire philosophy of apartheid was set out in the typical Verwoerdian style in the 1962 opening address:

The new nations were mainly of Asian and African origin, and the former metropolitan powers were their guides to knowledge, prosperity and potential nationhood. Communistic propaganda, despite the enslavement of nations and individuals under communist control, took the line of depicting this development, for which the controlling powers were responsible, as a struggle for freedom, and more often as a struggle by non-Whites against White oppressors. The communist factor which is responsible for much of the frustration, incitement, hatred, attacks and slogans, so rife in the world to-day, often shelters behind humanistic, liberal and moral propaganda.

It is against this international background that the difficulties which face the Republic of South Africa must be seen. Those in charge of its affairs must maintain law and order within its borders, when these tendencies make themselves felt here. They must oppose by every means at the Republic's disposal, any attack, in whatever form, upon the integrity of the State, particularly campaigns deriving from forces which allegedly pursue the path of peace and coexistence, but which in practice seek the destruction of the legitimate rights of communities, and even of nations with different identities. Those in charge of the Republic's affairs must more particularly continue, with zest, the implementation of its own solution for providing a genuine political future for all its racial groups.

This, in fact, is the most important issue with which the Republic is faced in the international field. In all other matters its good intentions are fundamentally unquestioned. Wherever the Republic has to meet pressure or attack – whether in regard to South West Africa or the Republic itself – it is related to

7

the matter of political rights. The form which the pressure takes is stated un-ambiguously, namely full political franchise for all. The objective is equally clear, namely that Southern Africa and the whole of Africa must be ruled by Black peoples. The main force behind this aim should also be stated frankly, namely the communist policy of world domination.

What course must South Africa follow? There is the path of expediency. Expediency would not, however, be served by minor measures. Experience elsewhere in Africa has shown that neither the demands of the Afro-Asian bloc, nor the instigations of the communist groups, would be satisfied by any-thing less than full acceptance of a policy of 'one man one vote' in one multi-racial state and therefore the recognition of majority rule by the Black voters. Any political system to retain White control in a professedly multi-racial state – however subtly contrived, and even if put forward as an intermediary step to Black rule in the future – would diminish neither the attacks nor the pressure and uncertainty. Some Western nations might wish to satisfy themselves and others with so-called concessions, whether in regard to South West Africa or the policy of separate development. If, however, they should find, as they will, that this does not appease those Afro-Asian states which they court as possible allies in the cold war, then, until disillusioned by other events, they will most likely feel compelled to follow in exèrting further pressure.

The path of expediency must therefore lead to political and, in fact, to na-tional suicide for the White nation in South Africa. It will also result in economic disaster for Whites, Coloured and Bantu. Whether the method of quick surrender is followed or recourse is had to rearguard action, the result would be inevitable. Justice for the White man in South Africa will have been sacrificed. For a time the Western nations may find comfort in the belief that a problem has been removed. For Communism, however, an objective more satisfactory than any of its successes elsewhere against the West, will have been achieved. Sooner or later, through the deterioration or chaos which must follow, the whole of Africa could be dominated, its wealth exploited, the seaway between East and West controlled, and the shrinking West hopelessly encircled.

For the Republic of South Africa the path of expediency in any form is therefore quite impossible, both as a matter of national survival and as the duty of a loyal member of the West in the struggle against world Communism.

The only alternative is the road of national reconstruction based on differen-tiation and with due regard to the interests of the different sections of the population.

Good race relations must therefore be a prime objective of national policy. In addition, it is clear that this will not be achieved by White domination, as the result of our present status or skill, over all non-Whites as a permanent aim in one common multi-racial fatherland; nor will good race relations be achieved by Black domination, as the result of their numerical superiority, over all smaller groups in such a multi-racial state. In order to establish peace

8

and tranquility and harmonious relations, each racial unit must therefore be guided, in accordance with a clear pattern, to a form of self-government suited to it.

The task on which the Government will therefore concentrate, while continuing as guardian with its broader administration, will be to adapt economic development, systematically and as fast as possible, to coming circumstances. It wishes to train and exercise the necessary leaders within each racial group to serve their own people. It further wishes, in consultation and co-operation with their authorities, to promote the process of emancipation of the Bantu from their familiar traditional systems to democratic self-government. The Government's purposeful policy in this connection is thus not suppression or discrimination based on race or colour, as has been alleged, but in fact its removal by the separation of the White and Bantu communities. This must be accompanied by granting to each the fullest rights in its own area, as well as imposing the same limitations on each in the area of the other.

(*Hansard*, January 19, 1962.)

Negotiation, too, was once again on the cards:

The major matter with which Parliament and the people will thus be concerned, will be how to grant self-government to the Bantu as speedily as they themselves wish and are able to accept it. This will have to be done in such a way as to allow these communities to function on a healthy, efficient and truly democratic basis, and so as to ensure the maintenance of friendship and co-operation with the Whites. Thus the position of the Whites will at the same time be safeguarded.

Jointly with this process, provisions will have to be made even at this stage, on an organized basis, for mutual consultation and co-operation with the new authorities in matters of common concern. Administration, and legislation where necessary, will have to be concentrated upon this sphere of new political growth.

(*Hansard*, January 19, 1962.)

International revolt against this policy was also foreseen:

In spite of everything being done and still to be done towards positive development and the clarification of South Africa's case, a blind eye should not be turned – in the light of what is happening in the world – to the dangers which may threaten its full development as a nation or even the survival of the State. The Republic must take into account the unjustified demands and pressures which may come from within the country or from outside as a result of the specific ideological struggle to which reference has already been made. Adequate provision will thus have to be made for internal security, and the necessary steps continued to ensure the effective defence of the country.

(*Hansard*, January 19, 1962.)

The 1966 opening address again referred pointedly to attempts to undermine stability and resist legislation aimed at combating subversion and treason (*Hansard*, January 21, 1966). Of developments in the Transkei it was stated with great confidence:

Those who feel themselves called upon to criticize could well learn from the success of South Africa in achieving harmony between races – in a land of many races – through the mutual recognition and appreciation of each other's national characteristics, culture and qualities.

(*Hansard*, January 21, 1966.)

The opening address of 1967 had to call yet again for further measures to contain sabotage, terrorism, agitators and incitement (*Hansard*, January 20, 1967), yet any fears were allayed with an arrogant pronouncement:

The implementation and development of the policy of separate or independent development finds increasing support with the Bantu. With the growth of their realization that the policy stems from an awareness on the part of the whites of their mission to develop a form of co-existence that presents the opportunity to each separate nation to realise themselves and to contribute to the prosperity of the country according to their ability, their confidence in the policy is stimulated. Likewise, mutual relationships and a spirit of constructive co-operation are promoted.

(*Hansard*, January 20, 1967.)

In 1968 it was reported that attempts from abroad to disturb the peace by means of terrorists had failed abjectly (*Hansard*, February 2, 1968).

These themes run like a refrain through the *Hansards* of parliamentary opening addresses from 1971 to 1974: incitement by subversive organizations, subversive activities bent on violent social, economic and political change; warnings that domestic peace should not inspire a false sense of security; pressure groups committed to revolutionary political activities; and a low-intensity war against South Africa.

The 1977 and 1978 opening addresses were made amidst the large-scale tensions of domestic unrest:

It may justifiably be said that 1976 was a watershed year for the Republic of South Africa, a year characterized on the one hand by far-reaching developments on the international scene and on the other by the emergence within the

Republic of elements who believe that the attainment of meaningful political rights for all our peoples is only possible by totally destroying, if need be through violence and bloodshed, the existing political, economic and social order.

...

Unmistakable though the underlying political motive is, it is ironic that in the very year when the Government carried its policy of separate freedoms through to its logical consequences, first with the granting of independence to the Republic of Transkei, to be followed shortly by Bophuthatswana, the forces of subversion instigated widespread riots, particularly in Bantu and Coloured residential areas, which led to senseless destruction of property, tragic loss of life, and disruption of the community life of the peace-loving majority.

Although the police displayed the utmost restraint during the rioting, at times in extremely dangerous situations, they were often compelled to use force in order to protect lives and property and to restore order.

(*Hansard*, January 21, 1977.)

Joint consultation was offered as a strategy to resolve the tension (*Hansard*, January 21, 1977), and the 1978 opening address offered Parliament the well-known rationalization:

The Government considers the most effective counter to the destructive criticism and the subversive attacks on us to be the upliftment of all the inhabitants of our country, the improvement of their social conditions and material welfare, and the institution of a political dispensation which will be fair and just to every population group, without losing sight of the realities of the South African situation. It is the Government's intention to continue on this tried and true course.

(*Hansard*, January 27, 1978.)

From 1979 to 1989, opening addresses were patently trying to counter revolt with the P W Botha government's well-known reform measures. The *Hansards* of that era record that constitutional changes to break away from the Westminster system were being planned for whites, coloured people and Indians; community councils were giving urban blacks a greater say in their own affairs; the consolidation of the homelands was receiving priority; a commission was to scrutinize security legislation; the Wiehahn Commission's report on industrial and labour relations had been released; the President's Council was established; a constellation of states and confederation were offered as models for co-operation; the grievances of black communities and aspects of discrimination were being addressed; fully-fledged black local managements were being set up; the concept of joint responsibility was enshrined in statutory structures for matters of common interest; uniform identity documents were introduced for all population groups; consensus politics was foreseen in a system of consociation; a special cabinet committee was appointed to decide on priorities for social, economic and constitutional development; structures for political participation by blacks – outside the Tricameral Parliament – were envisaged, albeit still on the basis of autonomy in the case of each group's own affairs and joint deliberation on matters of common interest; South African citizenship for all blacks; full freehold rights for black communities; the repeal of pass laws and influx control; acceptance of the principle of a unitary South African state and the right of all to vote (on racially segregated voters' rolls) for their elected representatives in the government of the country; power-sharing between all communities, but with the rights of groups protected; the proposed founding of a national statutory council for black communities to advise the government on political structures for blacks; an undertaking to release Mandela on humanitarian grounds, provided he rejected violence.

Despite all these announcements and developments – and numerous other reform measures that have not been listed here – a constant theme of opening addresses in those years was the unrest in the country and the security forces' successes in quelling it. Unrest was repeatedly blamed on an onslaught against the Republic's democratic lifestyle, a line of argument exemplified in the following statement:

The unrest in Black urban areas cannot be ignored. It must, however, be emphasized that steps will continue to be taken against those who promote violence and lawlessness. There is clear evidence that the vast majority of the residents of these areas support the Government's action to maintain order and are themselves begining to oppose the element of crime and violence that is thwarting efforts to improve the quality of life and participation in political processes.

At the same time the Government acknowledges that there are certain problems that lead to frustration in Black communities. The elimination of

12

these problems is receiving urgent attention so as to create better prospects for all. No responsible South African can lose sight of the fact that in the final instance the security of our country depends on the willingness of all our people, despite the considerable diversity, to accept that we have common interests and goals.

(Hansard, January 25, 1985.)

By declaring a national state of emergency in 1986, the gauntlet was taken up with a vengeance, as this portion of the 1987 opening address indicates:

The continuing unrest and violence in some of the Black residential areas remained the cause of unnecessary suffering and loss of life in 1986. We deeply regret every drop of blood spilt as a result of political violence.

Although the internal security situation improved initially, the unrest began to assume more serious proportions towards the middle of 1986.

Consequently, the Government was obliged to impose a nation-wide state of emergency. The correctness of this course of action has been substantiated by the decline in the occurrence of incidents of unrest since then. The revolutionary climate, however, necessitates the continued maintenance of these measures of control.

On both sides of the political spectrum there are people who have a simplistic view of the causes of the unrest situation and the means of dealing with it.

On the one hand there are those who say the Government and its policies are the cause of the violence.

On the other hand there are those who see violence merely as the work of a few instigators.

From ANC documents recently obtained by the Government, it appears beyond doubt that the ANC/Communist alliance is endeavouring to incite the Black communities, not only against one another, but also against the Whites in South Africa. It is evident that the ANC/Communist alliance is encouraging racial violence – even though it could lead to bloodshed on a large scale. This terrorist savagery must be resisted.

The point of view that a paradise on earth can be achieved by violent revolution is nothing but a dangerous and totally naive dream. Those who wish to destroy the existing orderly system have not as yet come up with an answer that could provide South Africa with an improved dispensation.

It is impossible to create an ideal society overnight, especially not one as complex as South Africa.

Nobody should be misled by the fine phrases with which the ANC/Communist Party alliance has been seeking recognition and respectability at home and abroad in recent times. Discussions with the ANC are possible only if it severs its ties with and terminates its subservience to the Communist Party;

13

abandons violence; and participates, as peaceful South African citizens, in constitutional processes in South Africa.

I am convinced that the vast majority of South Africans of all groups are basically peace-loving people with a sense of justice.

At the same time I must warn those who have committed themselves irrevocably to the violent overthrow of the State and the disruption of society, that the Government will not for a moment hesitate to act decisively against them.

The Government would like to lift the state of emergency, but will maintain its basic responsibility to purposely uphold law and order at all times.

(*Hansard*, January 30, 1987.)

3

In defiance of growing international isolation and domestic unrest, apartheid had in fact been built up systematically over 41 years, and the crisis had mounted year after year.

Having collated these summaries of the opening addresses of 41 years I submitted them to F W for comment. The crux of his succinct comment was the following:

'Already in the seventies and especially in the eighties it had become clear that the National Party had to make a fundamental change of course. It was done step by step and the 1987 election put the seal on it. In the meantime the urgency for quick implementation of new directions had built up. The motivating force behind my first opening address was precisely that urgency from abroad and at home. Months before the time I had become convinced that something drastic needed to be done, and it is that need that the speech of February 2, 1990, tried to address.'

4

As the time approached for the opening address on February 2, 1990, suspense and expectation became nearly palpable.

The press gallery in Parliament was packed to capacity, and not a seat was vacant in the public gallery, where selected guests were accommodated. The ambassadors of various countries were at their posts. Television teams from all quarters of the

14

world occupied every permissible spot in the chamber, and 200 press organizations were reported present.

What had occasioned such unwonted interest? The journalists had diverse motives, of course: the release of Mandela was expected at about the time of the opening of Parliament; the Mass Democratic Movement was planning a mass protest march under the banner 'Parliament must dissolve – Let the people govern'; that same week, attention had focused on protest marches and the water cannons, razor wire and police action that accompanied them; supporters of the 'struggle' were up in arms about the British rebel cricket tour of the country. Whatever the expectations, there was an air of extraordinary suspense – always a powerful magnet for the press.

Another reason for that interest was, undoubtedly, State President F W de Klerk himself. For weeks the national and foreign press had been speculating that he was going to make a major policy speech, and he himself had fuelled expectations.

Since his election as leader of the National Party a year before, to the day – on February 2, 1989 – and before and after his installation as State President on September 20, 1989, he had often surprised with his style and actions. In his inaugural speech he had committed himself and his government to active efforts to remove obstacles to negotiation, singling out five critical areas for attention: bridging the gap of distrust, initiating the process of negotiation, opening the door to economic prosperity, setting up a new political dispensation to accommodate everyone in the country, and dealing firmly with violence.

His track record included opening up beaches and public facilities to all races, allowing peaceful protest marches, releasing a group of political detainees, and drastically trimming government expenditure, including the defence budget.

To his credit he had a European and an African visit, which had received very favourable press reports. In general, his relations with the media had been relaxed, informative, pragmatic and flexible.

Spokesmen of the National Party, too, had made much of the positive expectations of a major speech.

But press reports and speculation had also produced some negative predictions. According to news reports of January 19, 1990, Mandela himself had told a delegation of the South African Youth Congress that he was placing no hopes on the address of February 2, for although De Klerk had made some changes he remained a National Party leader, trapped in apartheid, and was being unrealistic in his demand that violence be renounced and that all ties with the South African Communist Party be broken.

It was pointed out that National Party reforms, limited as they were, had all too often dashed any high hopes. De Klerk, it was written, could not risk taking any daring leaps since he would have to be mindful of his own power-base, which was being eroded by defections to the Conservative Party; extra-parliamentary and international audiences should not expect too much of him. It was feared that his speech would try to drive a wedge between Mandela and his power-base, a ploy that would put the seal on F W's failure. Referring to his style of cautious, step-by-step reform, commentators concluded that his speech could hardly be expected to lend much momentum to the political process.

These negative expectations hinged on the fear that De Klerk, far from being an innovator, was a hidebound disciple of apartheid. It was even rumoured that he had tried to put brakes on all the reforms P W Botha had made. Among the pronouncements attributed to him were his advocacy of racial segregation in labour affairs; his denial that blacks had any right to permanent residence in white areas, and an appeal to whites to ensure that group areas and racial separation were maintained; his rejection of the concept of black trade unions; his insistence that the Group Areas Act was non-negotiable; his refusal to enter into any dialogue with the ANC and its sympathizers; and his warning to universities that he would reduce their government subsidies if they persisted in subversive political activities. All this was National Party policy at that time.

Spokesmen for various opposition groups urged him to take drastic action, even trying to prescribe the contents of his speech, yet few of them showed any real enthusiasm. At best, vague hopes were expressed.

In the days leading up to the opening, all and sundry had cautioned against a second 'Rubicon'. (In August, 1985, a disappointing policy speech by his predecessor, P W Botha, in Durban had caused a world-wide outcry, the value of the rand had plummeted overnight, shares fluctuated wildly, violence flared up all over the country, and international outrage reached an angry peak.)

Now, in the run-up to the 1990 opening address, the Rubicon spectre was abroad with a vengeance. The mood of nervousness was exacerbated by caveats even from government spokesmen, and the press, sensitive to such jitters, warned that there could be no instant solutions or panaceas. It was even suggested that expectations had been deliberately inflated by elements hoping to make political gain out of possible disappointments.

In the months before F W de Klerk's opening address, as in past years, two sets of expectations had grown up around him, one cautiously optimistic, the other cautiously pessimistic. The caution, in both cases, reveals something of the uncertainty surrounding De Klerk, and this uncertainty, it seems to me, was fed by two main factors: his public image as a conservative, and his public image as a 'flexible' rather than a 'rigid' politician.

The conservative image had many sources. F W is a party man, a veritable Mr National Party, and in that role he has always fought for party unity. Even when tension ran high between Andries Treurnicht and Prime Minister Vorster – and later President Botha – De Klerk kept striving for reconciliation, both behind the scenes and publicly. Some observers concluded, whether rightly or not, that he had sympathetic leanings towards the then ultra-conservative wing of the National Party; others, more charitably, saw him as a man holding the middle of the road because he was reluctant to commit himself to either side.

Once the split in the National Party had become irrevocable and the Conservative Party had consolidated itself, F W, as the Transvaal leader of the National Party, fought relentlessly against the Conservative Party. Nevertheless, he was still apt to make ultra-conservative noises in his attempts to halt the growth of the Conservatives; and if he was slowly edging towards a more enlightened stand, he was also constantly qualifying his pronouncements with what were seen as more 'balanced' ones, thus confirming suspicions that he was hedging his bets and trying to accommodate divergent perspectives.

In the past four years De Klerk has in fact come to spearhead the fight against the Conservative Party, so much so that he is now their most hated political adversary. But images and perceptions die hard, and the mantle of conservatism still clung to him. His election to the leadership of the National Party was by a meagre eight-vote majority over Barend du Plessis, the candidate of the enlightened element in the caucus – which suggests that even in the inner echelons of the party De Klerk was still not completely trusted as an enlightened politician. For years Pik Botha had been seen as the political leader of the enlightened element, and the in-fighting around Pik and F W had in fact been perceived as a struggle between the enlightened and the ultra-conservative factions in the party. When Pik was eliminated in the first round of the leadership ballot, his supporters promptly rallied behind Barend du Plessis.

De Klerk's actions after his election as party leader caught the enlightened movement in South Africa by surprise. They were unable to divorce him from his conservative history. However, within the National Party's inner circle a different opinion prevailed. Nevertheless, the mood in the days before his speech on February 2 remained cautious, whether optimistic or pessimistic.

His conservative image was reinforced by his speeches in and outside Parliament, which had as leitmotiv the National Party's concept of racial grouping. The refrain was that South Africa has four race groups – whites, blacks, coloureds and Indians; that these four groups are not, cannot be and may not be politically integrated; that the four should therefore be given separate institutions at all levels of government, from local to national; that each of the four groups should have its own communal institutions, including residential areas, schools and health services; that each group should have charge of its own affairs and elect its own representatives on separate voters' rolls, but that the four should join forces on matters of common interest – all of which would be dubbed 'power-sharing' and entrenched in segregated structures.

F W was one of the most forceful proponents of this policy. Although he was characteristically even-handed in his defence of segregation and common interests, the perception remained that he was putting stronger emphasis on the former: 'own affairs', self-preservation and self-determination were his mottoes. As leader of the white 'own affairs' administration, moreover, he became an advocate for white interests, thus projecting himself as Mr White as much as Mr National Party.

In private discussions between us this accent was strongly evident. He was indomitably opposed to and disturbed by my frequent confidential discussions with the ANC in London, for example, and over the years he also remained resentful of my conviction that the National Party's group concept was impracticable. When I relinquished my editorship of the Sunday paper *Rapport*, he explained in a television interview that my editorial line had deviated too far from the party's policies.

He certainly never formed part of the enlightened movement in South Africa.

As the National Party developed its reform policy under P W Botha's leadership, F W de Klerk grew with it. In fact, he was a co-architect and developer of the concept of power-sharing. The rumour that he obstructed P W Botha and Chris Heunis, then Minister of Constitutional Development, in their attempts to redirect policy is unfounded. In fact, he played a leading role in that shift, albeit strictly within the framework of official National Party policy. F W stood exactly in the centre, with no marked inclination to break out into any new frameworks.

That was yet another reason why there were misgivings about what he would have to say at the opening of Parliament on February 2, 1990.

It is worth mentioning three further sources of the ultra-conservative reputation that had become such an albatross around his neck.

On one occasion Pik Botha stated publicly that a black president for South Africa was a possibility. This stirred up a furore, especially because Pik failed to issue an acceptable correction through the press. As a result, P W Botha sharply reprimanded Pik in public. It was rumoured that F W had urged P W Botha to repudiate Pik, and De Klerk's speech in the House of Assembly immediately after the incident had strong conservative overtones. F W cautiously denied the role attributed to him, but the rumours did not die: he had gained the image of a man who obstructed progress.

The next label hung about him was that he had aborted P W Botha's Rubicon speech in 1985 by objecting that the policy statements were too extreme, too far to the left, and therefore unacceptable. This was a malicious rumour. F W had had a hand in the original text of the speech and had fully concurred with its contents. P W Botha himself had amended the text. What upset F W about the speech was, in his own words : 'It had been leaked abroad that P W was going to announce far-reaching reforms, which had aroused feverish expectations. If that had not happened, the speech would have been well received abroad. The leak and the exaggerated expectations negated and neutralized such positive elements as there were in the speech, both here and abroad.'

Be that as it may. I am convinced that the charges against F W in respect of the Rubicon speech were false, but the perception lived on.

A third reason for F W's conservative image was widespread speculation that his wife, Marike, was an ultra-conservative, a racist, a chauvinist set on elevating the Afrikaners to some kind of *Herrenvolk*, and an outspoken disciple of apartheid who objected in principle to any of the so-called reform measures; secretly, it was surmised, she was in sympathy with the Conservative Party. And worst of all: her influence on F W was so overbearing that she was in fact ruling the roost. Such rumours were common.

20

These allegations need a good deal of qualification. True, she is a conservative person with strong and outspoken views, and some of her recorded statements have a right-wing ring to them. Like F W, she had her ultra-conservative phases; but she, too, had grown with the National Party's reform policies and had loyally supported the numerous reformulations of the party's policy. She is now a firm proponent of the New South Africa, a role she plays with sincere conviction. That she holds the reins is gossip, pure and simple. She admires and deeply respects F W and fully concurs with his initiatives. She is a woman who knows her own mind and does not hesitate to make her contribution – a valuable one – but not as a censor or initiator of government policy.

F W said of her, 'Marike is a valuable, sensitive and intelligent sounding-board with whom I can share and test my thoughts. She helps me to sharpen my own thinking and intuition. She and I are basically of one mind about the political course we have to take.'

Despite evidence to the contrary, however, she was made out to be F W's ultra-conservative counsellor, and this, too, put a question mark over his opening address.

Apart from his conservative image, his personality was an unknown quantity. His public image was that of a man who sought compromise rather than confrontation. He was seen as a peacemaker, as the man with the apologetic smile and the soft touch, whose play on words suggested that he was trying to be all things to all men. It was said that he did not have the strength to strike out, that he was a conformist rather than a leader, a follower rather than a pioneer, a formulator of others' thoughts and not an entrepreneur of ideas. And so there were many who feared that he was not going to make the grade.

What follows in this book will be my personal assessment of F W, but I can state objectively that his perceived profile is contradicted by his track record as a resolute man who states his case with cordial frankness. According to his colleagues, in the last years of P W Botha's reign he was among the fearless few who did not hesitate to beard the lion in his den. Those same colleagues testify to his quick grasp of problems, his acute insight into possible solutions, and his lucid motivation of his chosen options. In this alone, they maintain, his ability as a leader is indisputable.

What is my evaluation of F W de Klerk's conservative image and 'flexible' personality?

Let me admit it: I, too, was on tenterhooks. Over the past two years, each of the highlights in his career drew a sigh of grateful relief from me, because I saw him as balancing on a knife-edge. Although our contacts over the past year had strengthened my hopes that he was going to deploy 'the other F W', I was astounded and surprised time and again. As I watched his 'conversion', step by step, I couldn't believe my ears at some of the things he told me in confidence.

Indisputably, F W has undergone a 'political conversion', but it was by no means a dramatic event; his conversion was built, rather, on pragmatism – it evolved as a process.

My conviction that he was heading for a political conversion was founded on six perceptions.

He had deliberately built up a conservative image and a flexible profile. In Afrikaner politics, power is based on conservative thinking; in the long run it gains you confidence, and once you have that, you can do magical things with the Afrikaner. That was F W's strategy, not rigid conservatism. He was pragmatic and ambitious enough to build his image on the middle course between enlightened and ultra-conservative, and he was astute enough to convert his basic reluctance to give offence into a personal style, a strategy that gained him acceptability and influence. Not that he dissimulated; he just followed his political intuition.

He holds faithfully to the rules of whatever pursuit he is engaged in. As an MP, as leader of the conservative Transvaal, and as a cabinet minister he had enough respect for his job to promote party policy without steeping himself in it or giving it messianic status as the only way, truth, or life. He is a jurist to the core, a stickler for precise interpretation.

He is a superb politician, which means that he keeps an ear to

22

the ground and is sensitive to the slightest tremors. On this quality I pinned my hopes: he would be responsive to the Barend du Plessis vote that had nearly cost him the party leadership. He might never admit this, but it must have been an edifying shock to him to discover that there was a hankering within the National Party for a truly innovative approach to politics. Sensitive to vibrations, he must have registered the pressure of enlightenment in the Afrikaner establishment. My initiatives as founding convener of the Democratic Party gave him sleepless nights, figuratively speaking, and made him tot up how many influential young Afrikaners were on the point of breaking ranks with the National Party. He would have registered that enlightened views had gained credence over the years because they were the views of a corps of Afrikaners, businessmen, young people, and some of the media. He would register that some members of his cabinet had had enough of dribbling and trickling changes. I pinned my hopes on F W the politician.

He is a highly intelligent, open-minded and educated man, which made me confident that he would listen and think, would weigh and measure and adapt critically, and would test his thinking against carefully selected factions. That has in fact happened.

He is an honest man, that I know, and it made me sure that in his new offices he would bring his characteristic sense of realism to bear on our country's problems. I know F W as a balanced, self-critical and highly realistic man. His attitude to life is serious, directed towards the truth, and rooted in a sense of responsibility. His leitmotiv is justice and fairness. I was convinced that these qualities would make him take a new look at South Africa, that they would open his eyes, and that they would lead him to clarity.

He is a relaxed man, whose strength lies in his ordinariness. I sensed that his personality might produce precisely those qualities of leadership that we needed at this juncture in our history; that his humility, his cordiality, his striving for harmony and compromise, his refinement and courtesy, his total lack of extremism and his aversion to the display of brute force would win the day. He is *primus inter pares* – first among equals – and that makes him eminently qualified to meet the demands of the nineties in South African politics.

5

The time has come to hear what F W himself has to say about his conservative image. In an interview with me he said:

'One feature of my approach is that I must do well whatever I am doing. In my political career I have often written myself a job description. As a backbencher, I saw my task as making a good speech and concentrating on the political in-fighting in Parliament. Formulating policy was not my job.

'The silver thread throughout my career was my advocacy of National Party policy in all its various formulations. I refrained from adjusting that policy or adapting it to my own liking or convictions. I analysed it as it was formulated, to the letter.

'Incorrectly, I gained an ultra-conservative image. I never formed part of a political school of thought, and I deliberately kept out of the cliques and foments of the enlightened and conservative factions in the party. If the policy I propounded was ultra-conservative, then that was the policy; it was not necessarily I who was ultra-conservative. I saw my role in the party as that of an interpreter of the party's real median policy at any stage. Being loyal to the party and true to my self-imposed task, I avoided using dialectical subtleties to give party policies an ultra-conservative or an enlightened twist to suit either my own inclinations or those of my audiences.

'When I became Transvaal leader of the National Party I gave myself a new job description: to play more and more of a leading role in policy formulation within the inner echelons of the party. And no one in the cabinet collaborated more closely with Chris Heunis on formulating policy for a future political dispensation than I did. I took part in numerous think-tanks, smaller committees, co-authored speeches and statements – all part of the design, adjustment, development and renewal of policy.

24

'When those of us in the inner circles – courageously led by P W Botha – had reached the conclusion that our policy had to shift from separate development to power-sharing, I gave it my full support. I want to put this very strongly: once we had gone through the process of reassessment I took a leap in my own mind, more decisively than many other National Party politicians, that power-sharing with blacks was the right course for a new political dispensation. From then on – for example in the 1987 election – I was the one who stuck my neck out furthest to sell that idea all over the country. I made it emphatically clear that the logical consequence of our policy was the inclusion of blacks in any new political system. This proves that my image as an ultra-conservative national leader of the party was false, a distorted image.

'Now that I am State President I have set myself a new job description, which is to draw the line of political power-sharing with blacks to its logical conclusions.'

6

Let us get back to the State President taking his stand on the rostrum for that opening address to Parliament.

The text of his speech on February 2, 1990, is a fairly bulky document of 20 pages. It had taken a great deal of effort, actually about 20 years of work. But let us leave that for later.

What had been the immediate run-up to that address? Again, let me give it in the form of an interview with F W de Klerk.

When did the leaps of February 2 crystallize in your mind?

'By the end of 1989 it had become more and more clear to me that the government's emphases had landed us in a dead-end street. Even now I have no doubts about the basic philosophy of the policy as formulated under P W Botha, but the way in which it was executed had become counter-productive. One must hold on to the initiative, and a policy must be capable of producing results and progress. We had to escape from a corner where everything had stagnated into confrontation.'

Did your religious sensitivity and philosophical principles help to push you over the line?

'One of my philosophical convictions is that no lasting solutions can be built on injustice. During my legal training at the University of Potchefstroom I became accustomed to thinking in terms of legal principles. I do not want to give my insights the status of God-given verities; that kind of thing has been misused too often in history. But I searched and prayed, and I believe God gives insight through human thought and emotions.'

Did you initiate everything in the speech? I am referring especially to its political aspects.

'I could never say that. It was a matter of teamwork and interaction, and later it became impossible to trace who had contributed what. It was a process.'

What do you mean by a process?

'We – the cabinet – began by asking ourselves how we could normalize the political process. The concept of initiative and high moral ground became a theme. We considered anew how you could absolutely justify what you were doing. That was when an intensive process began. Proposals were tossed around; cabinet committees examined aspects of possible actions; every minister debated the pros and cons of certain options. We tried to anticipate what could go wrong or right if we decided this or that. In the process things ripened rapidly, grew corporatively among us. But it was very hard work. Nothing was done on the spur of the moment. I myself was, of course, very ready for that leap.'

Was there any outside pressure for that leap?

'No. I would rather speak of the pressure of insights and opportunities. We had to release Mandela. The previous State President as well as Minister Kobie Coetsee and certain officials had prepared the ground. Mandela had committed himself to peace and P W Botha had accepted that and abandoned his demand that Mandela renounce all violence. In consequence we merely had to round off his release. I do not claim any credit for that ... but I did take the chance.

'The insight and opportunity to unban prohibited organizations, including the ANC, coincided with the logical conclusion that such a step would mean political normalization. In any event, many organizations were already busy promoting their policies and ideals. At the same time, the decline and collapse of communism in Eastern Europe and Russia put a new complexion on things. The ANC was formerly an instrument of Russian expansionism in Southern Africa; when that threat fell away, the carpet was pulled from under the ANC; its base of financing, counselling and moral support had crumbled.

'It was as if God had taken a hand – a new turn in world history. We had to seize the opportunity.'

Does that mean you thought the ANC was on its knees? Surely that would be a negative reason for unbanning them, rather than a positive consideration to normalize politics?

'Absolutely not. We knew that the ANC enjoyed wide support and that they had to be included in negotiations. The risk that the ANC was being used as a Trojan Horse by a superpower had drastically diminished.

Were there any other insights that persuaded you to take the leap?

'Yes. Before my election as State President I had visited England, Germany, Portugal and Italy, as well as a number of African leaders. It became abundantly clear to me that the restoration of international relations was within our grasp. Africa – Southern Africa – I felt, was reaching out to us. The trend is away from socialism. They are hankering after prosperity and peace. They, and the rest of the world, were looking to South Africa to help raise the subcontinent from its misery. I know they are still very hostile to us; I am not naive. But the doors are open, and they can stay open and open wider only if we take the initiative – and hold it – by the creation of a just dispensation.

'I should mention that Buthelezi and I had also broken the existing stalemate even before February 2, 1990. Both he and other black leaders felt strongly that the ANC should be unbanned before they could freely become part of the negotiation process.'

Wasn't the speech also a gambit to make negotiation more attainable?

'Of course. We had paid serious attention to the Harare document and its conditions for negotiation. Certain valid stumbling blocks were identified to which we did want to give attention. With me, negotiation is written in capital letters.'

Wasn't your speech a response to foreign threats?

'In no way. There were no pressures or threatening messages, merely the stated conviction that we ourselves held the key to normalizing our international relations.'

Were the contents of the speech first cleared, so to speak, with other concerns, for example the ANC?

'No, it was a government secret. We consulted only within our own ranks. It was not even submitted to the National Party caucus.'

Were the cabinet unanimous on the contents of the speech? Rumours are going around that there was hard bargaining, even tension with the security establishment, or at least differences on emphases.

'That, I can tell you quite frankly, is nonsense. There were no schools of thought. What I said on February 2 was decided absolutely unanimously.'

Whether I accept everything F W had to say about events leading to the speech? Yes, I do. I have checked and rechecked with him. There have been – as one might expect of a politician – some overstatements and some understatements, but as it is written, so did it happen.

What pushed F W towards his political 'conversion'? People are still wondering about this. It is obvious to me that there is no single answer to the question. He himself is inclined to shy away from the idea of a political conversion, seeing it as an exaggerated, even sensationalistic, idea.

I do believe, with all the available evidence, that he did undergo a political conversion. Taking together everything already mentioned, and still to be mentioned, in this book, I can sum up the events leading to this 'conversion' as follows:

The first was when he came to the realization that power-

28

sharing with the blacks in South Africa was the only way to a political solution. This breakthrough came as early as 1986, when the Federal Congress of the National Party took a resolution to this effect. He took an active part in the formulation of the new policy.

The second was that after 1986 his convictions firmed and this new insight became part of his political policy, which resulted in the formulation of the National Party's five-year plan of that time.

The third was his election as leader of the National Party on February 2, 1989. This was a crucial moment because he had to put his own stamp on the policy. The breakthrough did not come on February 2, 1990, but on February 8, 1989, when he made his first speech as leader in Parliament. He relates how, in the preceding week, he had had to take some final decisions, which were spelt out in the February 8 speech: a total change in South Africa's goals; a South Africa free of the antagonism of the past, of domination and oppression, and that would find expression in a true democracy. Hope lay in the fact that a plan of action would be developed for the short, medium and long term: he would immediately address the genuine grievances hampering negotiation; he would direct his efforts towards normalizing international relations; white domination in politics would cease; any domination by either majority or minority would be prevented, and discrimination would be unacceptable – and he would try to do all this in as short a time as possible.

In this speech his conversion was confirmed by his political promises and declaration of intent.

The fourth event was the fruition of February 2, 1990. He recognized changes in East and West Europe, Africa and South Africa and knew that he had to make dramatic moves. Here F W conclusively showed his strength and the determination with which he acts once his decision is taken.

Fifth was undoubtedly the direct and indirect influence of colleagues within the National Party after his election as leader. Men such as Gerrit Viljoen, the political philosopher and experienced communicator, who was completely informed about black aspirations and frustrations; Pik Botha, for many years a fighter for enlightened politics and a qualified interpreter of foreign opinion; Barend du Plessis, with his finger on the pulse of South Africa's economy as it lay in the stranglehold of apartheid; Dawie de Villiers, champion of justice, and many others, formed a circle around F W. Iron sharpens iron: they too contributed to his 'conversion'.

7

The first words of the opening address were spoken at about 11.15 on Friday, February 2, 1990, and the whole speech took just over half an hour.

I watched F W closely as I listened to the TV broadcast. I kept up a running commentary: 'Watch it!'; 'no, that's too negative'; 'speak faster'; 'that could have been better put'. But knowing him, I could read his eyes and his voice and his smile. He was radiating confidence, almost total commitment; dignified self-assurance without a glimmer of hesitation; an awareness that he was deliberately making history; the calmness of a man who felt free to speak the truth; and humility.

Incidentally F W has rapidly developed into a media success. Earlier in his career he had a too apologetic smile and a too strained expression, especially when he was putting on a show of annoyance. He seemed to be thinking too hard about precisely the right replies. He has, of course, had some expert counselling, but that was a drop in the bucket. As I see it, his media transformation into a highly marketable man in front of the camera is attributable to two factors. First, he has internalized the authority of his office, which gives him a halo touch; and, second, his credibility has been enhanced by the sincerity and integrity of his message.

As seen through the camera that morning, reactions to the speech became rather entertaining: the excitement of Dr Zach de Beer, parliamentary leader of the Democratic Party, who just couldn't seem to believe his ears; or the dour pugnacity of Dr Andries Treurnicht, leader of the Conservative Party, whose normal deadpan expression and unamiable smile slowly made way for a nervous twitching around the mouth and eyes; or the swelling expanse of Allan Hendrickse's full-moon visage, as if the leader of the Labour Party now found his normal face just too small to convey the sweep of his heartfelt agreement.

Immediately after the adjournment F W attended an official reception given by the Speaker, following which he addressed the caucus of the National Party to test the climate. That evening at Westbrooke, official residence of the State President, he relaxed with Cape Town friends and mulled over the events of the day. Saturday he spent nailed to the telephone and, later, partying with Transvaal MPs at the Fernwood recreation club, as is customary. On Sunday morning – again true to tradition – he attended the Dutch Reformed service in the Groote Kerk. On Monday, the no-confidence debate began in Parliament.

When I asked him how he felt about all the reactions he had received over the weekend he answered spontaneously, 'I was overcome, grateful, deeply moved, and encouraged.'

8

Apart from the hundreds of telegrams, telephone calls and notes the State President received from foreign governments, the newspaper headlines had their own story to tell. Here is a small random sample:

'South Africa and the world rejoice', 'South Africa breaks through political sound barrier: a new dimension of hope', 'No more reason for violence', 'Politics open to all', 'New steps may open doors', 'Abandon petty politics' (*Die Burger*, February 3, 1990). 'New Era for South Africa. Tributes pour in from around the world' (*Cape Times*, February 3, 1990). 'A Rubicon crossed' (*Natal Mercury*, February 3, 1990). 'World welcomes F W's major step forward. Bush wants to review sanctions. Pope may visit' (*The Star*, February 3, 1990). 'Road of drastic change' (*Citizen*, February 3, 1990). 'NP mothballs old ideas' (*Rapport*, February 4, 1990). 'A page has been turned in history' (*Sunday Times*, February 4, 1990). 'Riding the tide of South Africa's newfound spirit of optimism' *(Business Day*, February 5, 1990).

Further reactions, as recorded by news reports and headlines in the three days following the opening address, also tell their own story: 'Buthelezi praises De Klerk's speech: now up to Blacks' *(Citizen)*, 'F W courageous – Van Zyl Slabbert' *(Citizen)*, 'Takes one's breath away, says Tutu' *(Die Burger)*, 'S P's speech "daring", says Mandela' *(Die Burger)*, 'De Klerk has broken the old Nat pattern' *(City Press)*, 'Press can now play rightful role' *(Sowetan)*, 'F W has saved South Africa, say business leaders' *(Beeld)*, 'A new beginning' *(Finance Week)*, 'No going back as F W risks political life' *(Sunday Star)*, 'Students and media applaud reforms by F W' *(The Argus)*. From abroad came similar responses: 'News of change like celestial music. F W's speech saluted by world leaders'.

Positive messages were received from President George Bush, Margaret Thatcher, Perez de Quellar, President François Mitterrand, President Mario Soares, President Kenneth Kaunda, the ministers of foreign affairs of Japan, Holland, Israel, Canada, and scores of others. From Paris even Breyten Breytenbach responded elatedly, and *Business Day* (February 7) reported in detail on the praises of *Pravda* and the Russian department of foreign affairs.

Almost the only gloomy notes were sounded by the Conservative Party: 'Dealing with ANC is treason' *(Die Patriot)*, 'F W naive about communists, says Dr Treurnicht' *(Die Patriot)*, 'Dr T calls for new election after F W's speech' *(Citizen)*.

A reading of all the hundreds of reports in the South African and foreign media shows up three trends in responses: positive, cautious, and negative.

The positive conclusions were that South African politics had been normalized, that most obstacles to negotiation had been removed, that the process had become irreversible, that F W was credible and had taken his first major step towards ultimate decisions, that South Africa's international isolation would now be reversed step by step, and that the democratization of South Africa would follow inevitably.

Cautious observers from certain foreign newspapers and

spokesmen for South African blacks concluded that F W still had a number of cards to put on the table: he had taken the easy steps, but the acid test would be his willingness to give content to a non-racial dispensation. Perhaps, it was speculated, he was simply a clever strategist who had caught his 'enemy', the ANC, with a deft ploy. He still had a long way to go, with many obstacles in his path.

The negative reactions came from two quarters: from black radicals responding with mistrust and even anger, claiming that this was just another gimmick by the engineers of apartheid; and from the right-wing movement in South Africa, who condemned the speech as the ultimate sell-out to the blacks, as an arrogant challenge to whites to start the revolution (since February white terrorism has in fact shot up sharply), and as a betrayal of the people, since the last election had given F W no mandate for such a speech.

Seen against the background of 41 years of Parliamentary opening addresses, against F W's conservative, middle-of-the-road image, against the National Party's track record, against many expectations and in confirmation of many others, the speech State President F W de Klerk made on February 2, 1990, was anything but a damp squib.

2

THE TURNING-POINT

1

In history, nothing comes out of the blue. F W de Klerk's opening address was the peak of a surge building up over many years, as a wave gathers momentum until it finally breaks on the shore.

The breaking of that wave is recorded in the *Hansard* of the Second Session of the Ninth Parliament of the Republic of South Africa.

STATE PRESIDENT'S OPENING ADDRESS

The STATE PRESIDENT: Mr Speaker, Members of Parliament:

The general election on 6 September 1989 placed our country irrevocably on the road of drastic change. Underlying this is the growing realisation by an increasing number of South Africans that only a negotiated understanding among the representative leaders of the entire population is able to ensure lasting peace.

The alternative is growing violence, tension and conflict. That is unacceptable and in nobody's interest. The well-being of all in this country is linked inextricably to the ability of the leaders to come to terms with one another on a new dispensation. No-one can escape this simple truth.

On its part, the Government will accord the process of negotiation the highest priority. The aim is a totally new and just constitutional dispensation in which every inhabitant will enjoy equal rights, treatment and opportunity in every sphere of endeavour – constitutional, social and economic.

I hope that this new Parliament will play a constructive part in both the prelude to negotiations and the negotiating process itself. I wish to ask all who identify yourselves with the broad aim of a new South Africa, and that is the overwhelming majority:

34

- Let us put petty politics aside when we discuss the future during this session.
- Help us build a broad consensus about the fundamentals of a new, realistic and democratic dispensation.
- Let us work together on a plan that will rid our country of suspicion and steer it away from domination and radicalism of any kind.

During the term of this new Parliament we shall have to deal, complementary to one another, with the normal processes of legislation and day-to-day government, as well as with the process of negotiation and renewal.

Within this framework I wish to deal first with several matters more closely concerned with the normal process of government before I turn specifically to negotiation and related issues.

FOREIGN RELATIONS

The Government is aware of the important part the world at large has to play in the realisation of our country's national interests.

Without contact and co-operation with the rest of the world we cannot promote the well-being and security of our citizens. The dynamic developments in international politics have created new opportunities for South Africa as well. Important advances have been made, among other things, in our contacts abroad, especially where these were precluded previously by ideological considerations.

I hope this trend will be encouraged by the important change of climate that is taking place in South Africa.

For South Africa, indeed for the whole world, the past year has been one of change and major upheaval. In Eastern Europe and even the Soviet Union itself, political and economic upheaval surged forward in an unstoppable tide. At the same time, Beijing temporarily smothered with brutal violence the yearning of the people of the Chinese mainland for greater freedom.

The year 1989 will go down in history as the year in which Stalinist Communism expired. These developments will entail unpredictable consequences for Europe, but they will also be of decisive importance to Africa. The indications are that the countries of Eastern and Central Europe will receive greater attention, while this will decline in the case of Africa.

The collapse, particularly of the Marxist economic system in Eastern Europe, also serves as a warning to those who insist on persisting with it in Africa. Those who seek to force this failure of a system on South Africa should engage in a total revision of their point of view. It should be clear to all that it is not the answer here either. The new situation in Eastern Europe also shows that foreign intervention is no recipe for domestic change. It never succeeds, regardless of its ideological motivation. The upheaval in Eastern Europe took place without the involvement of the Big Powers or of the United Nations.

The countries of Southern Africa are faced with a particular challenge:

Southern Africa now has a historical opportunity to set aside its conflicts and ideological differences and draw up a joint programme of reconstruction. It should be sufficiently attractive to ensure that the Southern African region obtains adequate investment and loan capital from the industrial countries of the world. Unless the countries of Southern Africa achieve stability and a common approach to economic development rapidly, they will be faced by further decline and ruin.

The Government is prepared to enter into discussions with other Southern African countries with the aim of formulating a realistic development plan. The Government believes that the obstacles in the way of a conference of Southern African states have now been removed sufficiently.

Hostile postures have to be replaced by co-operative ones; confrontation by contact; disengagement by engagement; slogans by deliberate debate.

The season of violence is over. The time for reconstruction and reconciliation has arrived.

Recently there have, indeed, been unusually positive results in South Africa's contacts and relations with other African states. During my visits to their countries I was received cordially, both in private and in public, by Presidents Mobutu, Chissano, Houphouet-Boigny and Kaunda. These leaders expressed their sincere concern about the serious economic problems in our part of the world. They agreed that South Africa could and should play a positive part in regional co-operation and development.

Our positive contribution to the independence process in South West Africa has been recognised internationally. South Africa's good faith and reliability as a negotiator made a significant contribution to the success of the events. This, too, did not go unnoticed. Similarly, our efforts to help bring an end to the domestic conflict situations in Mozambique and Angola have received positive acknowledgement.

At present the Government is involved in negotiations concerning our future relations with an independent Namibia and there is no reason why good relations should not exist between the two countries. Namibia needs South Africa and we are prepared to play a constructive part.

Closer to home, I paid fruitful visits to Venda, Transkei and Ciskei and intend visiting Bophuthatswana soon. In recent times there has been an interesting debate about the future relationship of the TBVC countries with South Africa, and specifically about whether they should be re-incorporated into our country.

Without rejecting this idea out of hand it should be borne in mind that it is but one of many possibilities. These countries are constitutionally independent. Any return to South Africa will have to be dealt with not only by means of legislation in their parliaments, but also through legislation in this parliament. Naturally this will have to be preceeded by talks and agreements.

HUMAN RIGHTS

Some time ago the Government referred the question of the protection of fundamental human rights to the South African Law Commission. This resulted in the Law Commission's interim working document on individual and minority rights. It elicited substantial public interest.

I am satisfied that every individual and organisation in the country has had ample opportunity to make representations to the Law Commission, express criticism freely and make suggestions. At present, the Law Commission is considering the representations received. A final report is expected during the course of this year.

In view of the exceptional importance of the subject of human rights to our country and all its people, I wish to ask the Law Commission to accord this task high priority.

The whole question of protecting individual and minority rights, which includes collective rights and the rights of national groups, is still under consideration by the Law Commission. Therefore it would be inappropriate of the Government to express a view on the details now. However, certain matters of principle have emerged fairly clearly and I wish to devote some remarks to them.

The Government accepts the principle of the recognition and protection of the fundamental individual rights which form the constitutional basis of most Western democracies. We acknowledge, too, that the most practical way of protecting those rights is vested in a declaration of rights justifiable by an independent judiciary.

However, it is clear that a system for the protection of the rights of individuals, minorities and national entities has to form a well-rounded and balanced whole. South Africa has its own national composition, and our constitutional dispensation has to take this into account. The formal recognition of individual rights does not mean that the problems of a heterogeneous population will simply disappear. Any new constitution which disregards this reality will be inappropriate and even harmful.

Naturally, the protection of collective, minority and national rights may not bring about an imbalance in respect of individual rights. It is neither the Government's policy nor its intention that any group – in whichever way it may be defined – shall be favoured over or in relation to any of the others.

The Government is requesting the Law Commission to undertake a further task and report on it. This task is directed at the balanced protection in a future constitution of the human rights of all our citizens, as well as of collective units, associations, minorities and peoples. This investigation will also serve the purpose of supporting negotiations towards a new constitution.

The terms of reference also include:

– the identification of the main types and models of democratic constitutions which deserve consideration in the aforementioned context;

- an analysis of the ways in which the relevant rights are protected in every model; and
- possible methods by means of which such constitutions may be made to succeed and be safeguarded in a legitimate manner.

THE DEATH PENALTY

The death penalty has been the subject of intensive discussion in recent months. However, the Government has been giving its attention to this extremely sensitive issue for some time. On 27 April 1989 the hon the Minister of Justice indicated that there was merit in suggestions for reform in this area. Since 1988, in fact, my predecessor and I have been taking decisions on reprieves which have led, in proportion, to a drastic decline in executions.

We have now reached the position in which we are able to make concrete proposals for reform. After the Chief Justice was consulted, and he in turn had consulted the Bench, and after the Government had noted the opinions of academics and other interested parties, the Government decided on the following broad principles from a variety of available options:

- that reform in this area was indicated;
- that the death penalty should be limited as an option of sentence to extreme cases, and specifically through broadening judicial discretion in the imposition of sentence; and
- that an automatic right of appeal be granted to those under sentence of death.

Should these proposals be adopted, they should have a significant influence on the imposition of death sentences on the one hand and, on the other, should ensure that every case in which a person has been sentenced to death will come to the attention of the Appellate Division.

These proposals require that everybody currently awaiting execution be accorded the benefit of the proposed new approach. Therefore all executions have been suspended and no executions will take place until Parliament has taken a final decision on the new proposals. In the event of the proposals being adopted, the case of every person involved will be dealt with in accordance with the new guidelines. In the meantime, no executions have taken place since 14 November 1989.

New and uncompleted cases will still be adjudicated in terms of the existing law. Only when the death sentence is imposed will the new proposals be applied, as in the case of those currently awaiting execution.

The legislation concerned also entails other related principles which will be announced and elucidated in due course by the Minister of Justice. It will now be formulated in consultation with experts and be submitted to Parliament as soon as possible.

I wish to urge everybody to join us in dealing with this highly sensitive issue in a responsible manner.

SOCIO-ECONOMIC ASPECTS

Constitutional reform implies far more than political and constitutional issues. It cannot be pursued successfully in isolation from problems in other spheres of life which demand practical solutions. Poverty, unemployment, housing shortages, inadequate education and training, illiteracy, health needs and numerous other problems still stand in the way of progress and prosperity and an improved quality of life.

The conservation of the physical and human environment is of cardinal importance to the quality of our existence. For this the Government is developing a strategy with the aid of an investigation by the President's Council.

All of these challenges are being dealt with urgently and comprehensively. The capability for this has to be created in an economically accountable manner. Consequently, existing strategies and aims are undergoing a comprehensive revision.

From this will emanate important policy announcements in the socio-economic sphere by the responsible Ministers during the course of the session. One matter about which it is possible to make a concrete announcement is the Reservation of Separate Amenities Act, 1953. Pursuant to my speech before the President's Council late last year, I wish to announce that this Act will be repealed during this session of Parliament.

The State cannot possibly deal alone with all of the social advancement our circumstances demand. The community at large, and especially the private sector, also have a major responsibility towards the welfare of our country and its people.

THE ECONOMY

A new South Africa is possible only if it is bolstered by a sound and growing economy, with particular emphasis on the creation of employment. With a view to this, the Government has taken thorough cognisance of the advice contained in numerous reports by a variety of advisory bodies. The central message is that South Africa, too, will have to make certain structural changes to its economy, just as its major trading partners had to do a decade or so ago.

The period of exceptionally high economic growth experienced by the Western World in the sixties was brought to an end by the oil crisis in 1973. Drastic structural adjustments became inevitable for these countries, especially after the second oil crisis in 1979, when serious imbalances occurred in their economies. After considerable sacrifices those countries which persevered with their structural adjustment programmes recovered economically so that lengthy periods of high economic growth and low inflation were possible.

During that particular period South Africa was protected temporarily by the rising gold price from the necessity of making similar adjustments immediately. In fact, the high gold price even brought great prosperity with it for a while. The recovery of the world economy and the decline in the price of gold and of other primary products brought with them unhealthy trends. These included high inflation, a serious weakening in the productivity of capital and stagnation in the economy's ability to generate income and employment opportunities. All of this made a drastic structural adjustment of our economy inevitable.

The Government's basic point of departure is to reduce the role of the public sector in the economy and to give the private sector maximum opportunity for optimal performance. In this process preference has to be given to allowing market forces and a sound competitive structure to bring about the necessary adjustments.

Naturally, those who make and implement economic policy have a major responsibility at the same time to promote an environment optimally conducive to investment, job creation and economic growth by means of appropriate and properly co-ordinated fiscal and monetary policy. The government remains committed to this balanced and practical approach.

By means of restricting capital expenditure in parastatal institutions and privatisation, deregulation and curtailing Government expenditure, substantial progress has already been made towards reducing the role of the authorities in the economy. We shall persist with this in a well-considered way.

This does not mean that the State will forsake its indispensable socio-economical development role, especially in our particular circumstances; on the contrary, it is the precise intention of the Government to concentrate an equitable portion of its capacity on these aims by means of the meticulous determination of priorities.

Following the progress that has been made in other areas of the economy in recent years it is now opportune to give particular attention to the supply side of the economy.

Fundamental factors which will contribute to the success of this restructuring are:

- the gradual reduction of inflation to levels comparable to those of our principal trading partners;
- the encouragement of personal initiative and savings;
- the subjection of all economic decisions by the authorities to stringent financial measures and discipline;
- rapid progress with the reform of our system of taxation; and
- the encouragement of exports as the impetus for industrialisation and earning foreign exchange.

These and other adjustments, which will require sacrifices, have to be seen as

40

prerequisites for a new period of sustained growth in productive employment in the nineties.

The Government is very much aware of the necessity for the proper co-ordination and consistent implementation of its economic policy. For this reason the establishment of the necessary structures and expertise to ensure this co-ordination is being given preference. This applies both to the various functions within the Government and to the interaction between the authorities and the private sector. The Government also notes with appreciation the way in which the Reserve Bank is carrying out its special responsibility in the pursuit of our common objectives.

This is obviously not the occasion for me to deal in greater detail with our total economic strategy or with the recent course of the economy. I shall confine myself to a few specific remarks on one aspect of fiscal policy that has been a source of criticism of the Government for some time, namely State expenditure.

The Government's financial year ends only in two months' time and several other important economic indicators for the 1989 calendar year are still subject to refinements at this stage. Nonetheless, several important trends are becoming increasingly clear. I am grateful to be able to say that we have apparently succeeded to a substantial degree in achieving most of our economic aims in the past year.

In respect of Government expenditure, the Budget for the current financial year will be the most accurate in many years. The financial figures will show:

- that Government expenditure is thoroughly under control;
- that our normal financing programme has not exerted any significant upward pressure on rates of interest; and
- that we will close the year with a surplus, even without taking the income from the privatisation of Iscor into account.

Without pre-empting this year's main Budget, I wish to emphasise that it is also our intention to co-ordinate fiscal and monetary policy in the coming financial year in a way that will enable us to achieve the ensuing goals, namely:

- that the present downturn will take the form of a soft landing which will help to make adjustments as easy as possible;
- that our economy will consolidate before the next upward phase so that we will be able to grow from a sound base; and
- that we shall persist with the implementation of the required structural adjustments in respect, among other things, of the following: easing the tax burden, especially on individuals; sustained and adequate generation of surpluses on the current account of the balance of payments; and the reconstruction of our gold and foreign exchange reserves.

It is a matter of considerable seriousness to the Government, especially in this particular period of our history, to promote a dynamic economy which will

41

make it possible for increasing numbers of people to be employed and share in rising standards of living.

NEGOTIATION

In conclusion, I wish to focus the spotlight on the process of negotiation and related issues. At this stage I am refraining deliberately from discussing the merits of numerous political questions which undoubtedly will be debated during the next few weeks. The focus now has to fall on negotiation.

Practically every leader agrees that negotiation is the key to reconciliation, peace and a new and just dispensation. However, numerous excuses for refusing to take part are advanced. Some of the reasons being advanced are valid. Others are merely part of a political chess game. And while the game of chess proceeds, valuable time is being lost.

Against this background I committed the Government during my inauguration to giving active attention to the most important obstacles in the way of negotiation. Today I am able to announce far-reaching decisions in this connection.

I believe that these decisions will shape a new phase in which there will be a movement away from measures which have been seized upon as a justification for confrontation and violence. The emphasis has to move, and will move now, to a debate and discussion of political and economic points of view as part of the process of negotiation.

I wish to urge every political and community leader, in and outside Parliament, to approach the new opportunities which are being created constructively. There is no time left for advancing all manner of new conditions that will delay the negotiating process.

The steps that have been decided on are the following:

- The prohibition of the African National Congress, the Pan Africanist Congress, the South African Communist Party and a number of subsidiary organisations is being rescinded.
- People serving prison sentences merely because they were members of one of these organisations or because they committed some other offence which was merely an offence because a prohibition on one of the organisations was in force, will be identified and released. Prisoners who have been sentenced for other offences such as murder, terrorism or arson are not affected by this.
- The media emergency regulations as well as the education emergency regulations are being abolished in their entirety.
- The security emergency regulations will be amended to continue to make provision for effective control over visual material pertaining to scenes of unrest.
- The restrictions in terms of the emergency regulations of 33 organisations

are being rescinded. These organisations include the following:
National Education Crisis Committee
South African National Students Congress
United Democratic Front
Cosatu
Die Blanke Bevrydingsbeweging van Suid-Afrika.
- The conditions imposed in terms of the security emergency regulations on
374 people upon their release are being rescinded and the regulations which
provide for such conditions are being abolished.
- The period of detention in terms of the security emergency regulations will
be limited henceforth to six months. Detainees also acquire the right to
legal representation and a medical practitioner of their own choosing.

These decisions by the Cabinet are in accordance with the Government's declared intention to normalise the political process in South Africa without
jeopardising the maintenance of good order. They were preceded by thorough
and unanimous advice by a group of officials which included members of the
security community.

Implementation will be immediate and, where necessary, notices will
appear in the *Government Gazette* from tomorrow.

The most important facets of the advice the Government received in this
connection are the following:

- The events in the Soviet Union and Eastern Europe, to which I have referred already, weaken the capability of organisations which were previously supported strongly from those quarters.
- The activities of the organisations in respect of which the prohibitions are
now being lifted no longer hold the same degree of threat to internal security which initially necessitated the imposition of the prohibitions.
- There have been important shifts of emphasis in the statements and points
of view of the most important of the organisations concerned, which indicate a new approach and a preference for peaceful solutions.
- The South African Police Force is convinced that it is able, in the present
circumstances, to combat violence and other crimes perpetrated also by
members of these organisations and to bring offenders to justice without
the aid of prohibitions on organisations.

About one matter there should be no doubt. The lifting of the prohibition on
the said organisations does not signify in the least the approval or condonation
of terrorism or crimes of violence committed under their banner or which may
be perpetrated in the future. Equally it should not be interpreted as a deviation
from the Government's stance in principle, among other things, against their
economic policy. This will be dealt with in debate and negotiation.

At the same time I wish to emphasise that the maintenance of law and order
dare not be jeopardised. The Government will not forsake its duty in this connection. Violence from whichever source will be fought with all available

43

might. Peaceful protest may not become the springboard for lawlessness, violence and intimidation. No democratic country can tolerate that.

Strong emphasis will also be placed on even more effective law enforcement. Proper provision of manpower and means for the police and all who are involved in the enforcement of the law will be ensured. In fact, the Budget for the coming financial year will begin to give effect to this.

I wish to thank the members of our security forces and related services for the dedicated service they have rendered the Republic of South Africa. Their dedication makes reform in a stable climate possible.

On the state of emergency I have been advised that an emergency situation which justifies these special measures which have been retained still exists. There is still conflict which is manifesting itself mainly in Natal, but also as a consequence of the countrywide political power struggle. In addition, there are indications that radicals are still trying to disrupt the possibilities of negotiation by means of mass violence.

It is my intention to terminate the state of emergency completely as soon as circumstances justify it, and I request the co-operation of everybody towards this end. Those responsible for unrest and conflict have to bear the blame for the continuing state of emergency. In the meantime, the state of emergency, as now amended, is inhibiting only those who use chaos and disorder as political instruments. Otherwise the rules of the game under the state of emergency are the same for everybody.

Against this background the Government is convinced that the decisions I have announced are justified from the security point of view. However, these decisions are justified from a political point of view as well.

Our country and all its people have been embroiled in conflict, tension and violent struggle for decades. It is time for us to break out of the cycle of violence and break through to peace and reconciliation. The silent majority is yearning for this. The youth deserve it.

With the steps the Government has taken it has proven its good faith and the table is laid for sensible leaders to begin talking about a new dispensation to reach an understanding by way of dialogue and discussion.

The agenda is open and the overall aims to which we are aspiring should be acceptable to all reasonable South Africans.

Among other things, those aims include a new, democratic constitution; universal franchise; no domination; equality before an independent judiciary; the protection of minorities as well as of individual rights; freedom of religion; a sound economy based on proven economic principles and private enterprise; and dynamic programmes directed at better education, health services, housing and social conditions for all.

In this connection Mr Nelson Mandela could play an important part. The Government has noted that he has declared himself to be willing to make a constructive contribution to the peaceful political process in South Africa.

I wish to put it plainly that the Government has taken a firm decision to release Mr Mandela unconditionally. I am serious about bringing this matter to finality without delay. The Government will take a decision soon on the date of his release. Unfortunately, a further short passage of time is unavoidable.

Normally there is a certain passage of time between the decision to release prisoners and their actual release because of logistical and administrative requirements. In the case of Mr Mandela there are factors in the way of his immediate release, not the least of which are his personal circumstances and safety. He has not been an ordinary prisoner for quite some time. Because of this his case requires particular circumspection.

Today's announcements in particular go to the heart of what Black leaders – also Mr Mandela – have been advancing over the years as their reason for having resorted to violence. The allegation has been that the Government has not wished to talk to them and that they have been deprived of their right to normal political activity by the prohibition of their organisations.

Without conceding that violence has ever been justified, I wish to say today to those who have argued in this manner:

– The Government wishes to talk to all leaders who seek peace.
– The unconditional lifting of prohibition on the said organisations places everybody in a position to pursue politics freely.
– The justification for violence which has always been advanced therefore no longer exists.

These facts place everybody in South Africa before a *fait accompli*. On the basis of numerous previous statements there is no longer any reasonable excuse for the continuation of violence. The time for talking has arrived and whoever still makes excuses does not really wish to talk.

Therefore I repeat my invitation with greater conviction than ever:

Walk through the open door and take your place at the negotiating table together with the Government and other leaders who have important power bases inside and outside of Parliament.

Henceforth everybody's political points of view will be tested against their realism, their workability and their fairness. The time for negotiation has arrived.

To those political leaders who have always resisted violence I say: Thank you for your principled stands. This includes all the leaders of parliamentary parties, leaders of important organisations and movements such as Chief Minister Buthelezi, all of the other Chief Ministers and urban community leaders.

Through their participation and discussion they have made an important contribution to this moment in which the process of free political participation is able to be restored. Their places in the negotiating process are assured.

CONCLUSION

In my inaugural address I said the following:

'All reasonable people in this country – by far the majority – anxiously await a message of hope. It is our responsibility as leaders in all spheres to provide that message realistically and with courage and conviction. If we fail in that, the ensuing chaos, the demise of stability and progress, will for ever be held against us.

'History has thrust upon the leadership of this country the tremendous responsibility to turn our country away from its present direction of conflict and confrontation.

'Only we, the leaders of our peoples, can do this.

'The eyes of responsible governments throughout the world are focused on us. The hopes of millions of South Africans are centred around us. The future of Southern Africa depends on us. We dare not falter or fail!'

This is where we stand:

– Deeply under the impression of our responsibility.
– Humble in the face of the tremendous challenges ahead.
– Determined to move forward in faith and with conviction.

I ask Parliament to assist me on the road ahead. There is much to be done.

I call on the international community to re-evaluate its position and to adopt a positive attitude towards the dynamic evolution which is taking place in South Africa.

I pray that the Almighty Lord will guide and sustain us on our course through uncharted waters and will bless our labours and deliberations.

MR SPEAKER AND HONOURABLE MEMBERS OF PARLIAMENT:

I now declare this Second Session of the Ninth Parliament of the Republic of South Africa to be duly opened.

2

This speech opened up a host of political perspectives.

It announced – conclusively – a truly new dispensation for South Africa: a dispensation of full democratization of the political system, of a universal franchise, of majority rule in a unitary state, of the protection of minorities, of an independent judiciary and equal justice for all under a human rights manifesto, of no discrimination, and of a free economy with restricted government control.

As a step towards that democracy the speech also announced

46

the normalization of political processes. The time when minorities dominated majorities was over. The freedom of the press was restored, the rule of law was recognized, and through the lifting of the emergency regulations the right of all political groupings to organization, affiliation, demonstration and protest was confirmed. Restrictions on political parties and figures were lifted and political detainees released. Security measures were depoliticized, beginning with the effective abolition of capital punishment and the prospect of a further purging of the country's security apparatus.

Democratization was the objective, the normalization of the political process was the means of achieving it, and a fully-fledged process of negotiation between the various political groupings was the method to be employed. Those negotiations – yet another notable breakthrough, given our historical background – would include all recognized groups within and outside Parliament.

Over the years South Africa has had two political systems. The so-called 'system politics' represented all groups that somehow formed part of the apartheid apparatus, including the parliamentary parties, the parliaments of the black national states, and representatives on local and regional governments. Parallel to that ran the so-called 'struggle politics' with such diverse groupings as the United Democratic Front, the Cosatu federation of trade unions, and a range of community organizations down to local levels. This 'struggle' was co-ordinated by the African National Congress (ANC) from its headquarters in Lusaka, Zambia.

The opening address suspended the division between these two systems by officially opting for an open agenda and thus scrapping all the old formulas, prerequisites, conditions and non-negotiables. The only framework is to be that of a Western democracy.

The heart of the speech, then, is its three pillars of democratization, normalization, and open negotiation. Further analysis, however, shows up some more decisive announcements.

By implication it was posited that South Africa's unity could be restored. Legal procedures were outlined whereby the TBVC countries (the independent apartheid states of Transkei, Bophuthatswana, Venda and Ciskei) could rejoin a unitary South African state. Thus it was tacitly admitted that apartheid's fragmentation of South Africa into separate, independent states had not succeeded; the philosophy on which everything had been built – 'Grand Apartheid', in National Party dialectics – had been scrapped.

The death knell of 'Petty Apartheid' – the segregation of races on all levels of society – was rung by the repealing of the Separate Amenities Act, and the few apartheid laws still in force were clearly on their way out. Discrimination – the speech stated – had been scrapped once and for all, and so had the racial element on which the whole apartheid policy had been founded.

Another leitmotiv of the speech was that the foundations of the state had been shifted from authoritarian to constitutional principles. Law and order remain essential to a constitutional state, but such a state is founded on the protection of the rights of individuals, groups, cultures and beliefs; majority participation is guaranteed, and minority participation is respected. Exclusivity (the right of free association and dissociation) and inclusivity (the equality of all before the law and government) are entrenched in a constitutional state. Through an independent judiciary, as final arbiter, government power is restricted by law.

This was the basic principle announced in the speech. The philosophy underlying the state to come under F W de Klerk had shifted from force to law. The additional instruction to the Law Commission of South Africa to design constitutional models for submission at future negotiations put those models, too – or at least their form and content – within the framework of a constitutional state.

The opening address also outlined a socio-economic strategy. The new state is to have a market-oriented economy, founded on the dynamics of private enterprise and the diminution of the government's role in economic control. At the same time, the speech committed the new state to large-scale development, in collaboration with the private sector, by giving priority to the elimination of housing shortages, inadequate education and training, unemployment, deficiencies in health services, and any other obstacles to progress, prosperity, and an enhanced quality of life. In principle, this meant a commitment to correcting the blacks' disadvantaged position in South Africa.

In terms of international relations, the speech was a breakthrough for South Africa. At the time South Africa was facing seven international crises: a crisis of morality, in that our political principles were rejected as immoral; a crisis of legitimacy, since our government had come to be seen more and more as the illegitimate regime of a minority over a majority; a crisis of credibility, since our political integrity was at issue; a crisis of security; the crisis of rejection, isolation and sanctions; the crisis of interference in our affairs; and the crisis of dwindling options.

A review of Koos van Wyk's doctoral thesis on South Africa's international situation came to the following conclusion (published in the *International Affairs Bulletin*, Vol. 11, No. 3, 1987):

Without doubt, South Africa's international position is closely related to and influenced by its domestic policies. Its position is in flux and is tied to the nature and tempo of internal change.

It is impossible to escape the fact that internationally South Africa is perceived as a pariah. The perceptions of the academic elite are arguably the most accurate. However, even South Africa's ties with other pariah states are in jeopardy. Israel is currently reviewing its close military links with South Africa because of pressure from the United States, thus potentially closing a vital channel for sophisticated technology. South Africa's relations to South American pariah states also hang in the balance. Regime changes from military governments to democracies in Brazil, Argentina and Peru have increased the vulnerability and illegitimacy of pro-South African regimes in Paraguay and Chile, although the stability of the transition in the case of the first two has yet to be determined and Chile can boast the only currently viable economy in South America. Increasingly, South Africa and Taiwan are becoming almost completely isolated from the international system, and their mutual trade and other agreements add up to very cold comfort.

Since this survey was conducted, the already acrimonious relations between South Africa and the West have deteriorated even further.

United States and other Western countries have distanced themselves from their recalcitrant former ally by introducing increasingly comprehensive and stringent trade sanctions against South Africa, driving the wedge between South Africa and the West ever more deeply, especially as the South African government's response has been to draw the 'laager' more tightly around the country.

Relations between South Africa and the West would only be normalised if majority rule could evolve or if truly sweeping reforms were to be initiated and carried through by the government.

In the same publication E Blumenfeld writes about sanctions, 'There is some evidence that the pendulum may be beginning to swing back, although my own assessment is that the momentum towards increasing economic isolation of South Africa from its traditional trading partners is still overwhelming' (p. 22).

In his speech, F W de Klerk made it clear that South Africa was ineluctably dependent on foreign relations for its well-being and security. Through his many announcements the ground had been prepared for a new international involvement in the development of the country. Moreover, his speech reiterated invitations to foreign entrepreneurs to contribute to the development of the subcontinent's self-sufficiency, free market, commerce and industry.

In an interview with me the State President had the following to say about his speech:

'In effect the speech was founded on the five-point plan for the 1989 election. I had a great deal to do with the formulation of that plan. We set five objectives, and I later added a sixth.

These were: the normalization of the political process, the removal of discrimination on the grounds of race, negotiation as a means of achieving a new constitutional dispensation, economic efficiency, the firm maintenance of law and order, and the removal of distrust and the building of bridges. These objectives were spelled out in my presidential address.

'On the question of South Africa's economic efficiency – one of those objectives – I should add that all future decisions will have to prove their economic viability. The state, too, will have to be managed efficiently. In addition, we shall have to address the problems of poverty and backlogs – far more so than in the past. Here the state will have to do whatever it can, for until the problems of backlogs have been addressed, no new constitutional dispensation could ever succeed. For that reason, a strong, vibrant economy is absolutely essential if we are to afford all the steps that will have to be taken to make up those backlogs.'

Further retrospective comment by F W de Klerk on his speech – I went through it with him again, paragraph by paragraph – included the following:

'To me, the concept of a constitutional state is of cardinal importance. Justice and the judiciary must be in a position to override power. Under no circumstances should it be possible to manipulate justice. And that has decided implications for arbitrary action, which could not be tolerated in such a state.

'Given our geographical and demographic diversity, I believe in elements of federalism for South Africa. The present national states would – with modifications – fit in very well as regional governments.

'I do not minimize the role of the security forces in a new South Africa. That perception is wrong; the accent has merely shifted. With the opening of Parliament, and the run-up to that opening, circumstances changed. The emphasis is no longer on the terrorist onslaught, on communist expansionism, on the hostility of African states and the risk of coups. Those things have levelled off. Now the security forces have to maintain normal law and order and defend our territorial integrity. But this is also a matter of my personal style. I am committed to the concept of government by cabinet, and the security forces are still playing an important role by providing briefing material for the cabinet's deliberations and decisions.'

3

De Klerk's opening address can indeed be described as a decisive, irreversible turning-point in the history of South Africa. One of its consequences was the public acknowledgement of the ANC's prominence in South African politics.

Over the years various strategies had been used to deal with the ANC. The first was to ignore it. The ANC has a long history of attempting to put its case to South African governments, only to have its pleas fall on deaf ears; in fact, most of them did not even receive a hearing.

The next strategy was to clamp down on the ANC in an attempt to strangle it to death. From 1950 to 1955 legislation and emergency measures were adopted to counter the ANC's passive resistance to apartheid. The upshot of all that friction was the convening of the Congress of the People on June 26, 1955, which adopted the well-known Freedom Charter as the ANC's political manifesto. On December 5, 1956, the government struck by charging a large number of people with high treason.

In the shocking events at Sharpeville and Langa in March, 1960, 69 people were shot and killed. A state of emergency was proclaimed and numerous arrests were made.

When it became clear that the ANC could not be smothered it was banned on April 8, 1960. Yet it kept gaining ground through its clandestine mobilization of support, by setting up front organizations to continue the struggle, and through acts of terrorism.

In South Africa the ANC became the symbol of the freedom struggle; abroad, it mustered wide support by setting up a network of missions that functioned virtually as embassies. Numerous opinion polls in the eighties confirmed that the ANC had mobilized the support of some 60 per cent of the black population.

Gradually, a new strategy was adopted by government: the ANC was demonized; it was represented as a front for the total onslaught of communism on all established South African values. Proclaimed a symbol of elemental evil, it was hunted down as in a full-scale war.

The next strategy was to minimize the ANC. The tenor of the propaganda against it was that its alleged support had been inflated, that its support had been extorted through intimidation and was therefore unreliable and that the 'silent majority' of moderate blacks supported the government. The ANC, it was argued, had eliminated itself as a factor to be reckoned with. Moreover, it was claimed, internal tension between the so-called nationalists and the communists in ANC ranks would further debilitate the movement.

Finally, an attempt was made to lure the ANC to rapprochement with the proposition that if it renounced violence, it would be invited to participate in a process of negotiation.

Then came F W de Klerk and his opening address. In the speech, as in the preceding months, the ANC was recognized as a legitimate, primary political force in South Africa. To encapsulate the *volte face* in one sentence, it was now accepted that the ANC formed part not of the problem but of the solution.

The ANC and its leaders were unbanned because it holds the key to reconciliation; in fact, the ANC is essential to the National Party's programme of renewal. Enmity, one might say, had sired a kind of partnership.

This is why the government has met many of the ANC's preconditions to negotiation, as set out in its Harare manifesto. Under the main heading 'Climate for Negotiations' that document stipulates:

Together with the rest of the world, we believe that it is essential, before any negotiations can take place, that the necessary climate for negotiations be created. The apartheid regime has the urgent responsibility to respond positively to this universally acclaimed demand and thus create this climate.

Accordingly, the present regime should, at the very least:

- release all political prisoners and detainees unconditionally and refrain from imposing any restrictions on them;
- lift all bans and restrictions on all proscribed and restricted organisations and persons;
- remove all troops from the townships;
- end the state of emergency and repeal all legislation, such as and including the Internal Security Act, designed to circumscribe political activity; and
- cease all political trials and political executions.

These measures are necessary to produce the conditions in which free political discussion can take place – an essential condition to ensure that the people themselves participate in the process of remaking their country. The measures listed above should therefore precede negotiations.

53

A consequence of the 'partnership' with the ANC was that the 'alliance' between the government and system politics had, at a stroke, lost all its prominence. The political influence of the coloured and Indian houses in Parliament was weakened, homeland leaders and local community leaders shifted to the background, and the hobnobbing with little groups of so-called moderates had suddenly become a thing of the past. Not that the partnership with system politics had disappeared; they are still involved in consultations.

F W's breakthrough with Buthelezi – there had been a wall between Buthelezi and P W Botha, whereas F W and the Inkatha leader had struck up a cordial relationship – is important but no longer primary. Inkatha is a political force, but through the opening address the ANC had become the main actor.

The speech still contained a few paternalistic and deprecating remarks about the ANC, perhaps to placate the white powerbase. Given events in Eastern Europe, it was claimed, the ANC had become part of a failed system; its capacity had been reduced and it now posed much less of a threat. Despite these afterthoughts, however, February 2 was a resounding triumph for the ANC. Its arch-enemy, the 'apartheid regime' – as it had consistently called the government – had recognized and accommodated its claim to being the major opposition group in the country.

Asked for his comment on this point, the State President confirmed my impression: 'The ANC is a fairly important element with a solid power-base among the people. Negotiations with others, without the ANC, would be incomplete, and their legitimacy questionable. I do not doubt for a moment that the ANC is prepared to compromise on the major issues. We must get away from the situation where the government is perceived to be abusing its powers for party-political purposes, by suppressing the ANC's political views.'

Here I must once again register astonishment. Hardly a year before (in 1989) this very man had sharply attacked me for holding talks in London with ANC leaders. I used to belong to a discussion group that held confidential talks with the ANC twice a year, and he had been outraged and disturbed by this 'hob-nobbing with terrorists'. Immediately after his inauguration on September 20, 1989 – that same afternoon, in fact – I went at his request to see a top man in the National Intelligence Service. At that meeting I had my arm twisted to stop visiting the ANC because it 'lent prominence to an organization on its knees', one that 'could never play a role in negotiations'.

F W's statement in *Beeld*, October 3, 1989, read as follows *(translated)*: 'No matter how well-intentioned these talks may be, the result is, generally, that the ANC and others exploit them to mask the intrinsic nature of revolutionary organizations and to promote an undeserved image of reasonableness. Thus participants in such talks are playing into the hands of forces that are still set on destabilizing South Africa and destroying law and order.'

F W de Klerk has truly undergone a major political conversion.

The reasoning of the time was that it could be very uncomfortable for the State President if his brother was seen to be his spokesman. The flaw in this argument was that I had been taking part in discussions for the previous two years. I am also completely convinced that the continuing discussions of our group helped set the scene for compromise and negotiation. Our meetings, as well as those of other groups that came together from time to time, were fruitful trail-breakers for what later followed.

4

A further consequence of that opening address was that it sent the already battered concept of apartheid reeling.

It has been asked whether the government might not still deviously try to uphold certain remnants of apartheid, for instance by enforcing the concept of the protection of minority rights through a form of racial federation. This will be dealt with later. What is beyond dispute, however, is that the speech on February 2, 1990, formally concluded the era of apartheid.

Apartheid was built on three pillars: first, territorial segregation on all levels of society, from separate states for each population group to the racial segregation of communities in residential areas, transport, schools, and any other conceivable human activity; second, a legislative programme that created the statutory web needed to make apartheid an enforceable ordination; and third, structures to draw together all the many states and groups for consultation on matters of common interest.

Through territorial segregation, it was planned, all population groups, especially the blacks, would eventually be assigned to separate states that could be developed into independent economic units. Industries set up on the borders of such states would provide employment to blacks, thus stimulating a reflux of blacks from the 'white areas' to their own territories. The international community, it was also hoped, would recognize these black states as independent countries. Black workers living in white areas were seen as 'migrant labourers' who had to exercise their political rights in their own states. Initially, the migrant labourers were regarded as transient 'boarders' and crammed into dormitory townships. These were never developed into viable residential suburbs; as makeshift compounds, they had to serve as a constant reminder of the migrant labourer's temporary status. Later, however, the permanency of blacks in 'white South Africa' was recognized (after lengthy political debate over many years). Through various consultative structures they were given local self-government, better township development, and better housing.

The entire concept was riddled with pitfalls, of which I shall mention only a few. The demand for black labour in the metropolitan areas of 'white South Africa' resulted in a virtually uncontrollable influx of black workers; the planned reflux to their own territories never developed, *inter alia* because the sparse border industries could not provide enough jobs and because poverty in the homelands aggravated the misery of the people; socio-economic development in the homelands was virtually non-existent, partly because the homeland budgets were hopelessly inadequate for such developments and partly because the poverty culture had virtually ruled out black entrepreneurship. The experiment with the independence of four states – Transkei, Bophuthatswana, Venda and Ciskei – flopped because they could not make the grade and because the international community refused to recognize their independence; resistance to this policy grew strongly in the homelands, and Buthelezi, the chief minister of KwaZulu, took a particularly firm stand against it; patches of the black states were sprinkled far and wide, and attempts to consolidate their territories made painfully slow progress; the entire homelands project became less and less affordable, *inter alia* because government departments were duplicated in each homeland; blacks in white areas began to distance themselves from the homelands and refused to be involved in their politics.

De facto, De Klerk's opening address put an end to the painful process of territorial segregation and replaced it with the concept of an indivisible, unitary South African state. In a new South Africa the homelands might be retained as regional entities, but no longer as black national states.

The legislative programme – the second leg of apartheid – was likewise a failure. Refusing to have their communal life confined to specific communities, South Africans blended together. Gradually – also after strong protest, much dispute and many confrontations – concessions were made: whites and non-whites were allowed to share facilities on certain levels, racially mixed sport was allowed here and there, and it was admitted that, beyond the black-and-white worlds, there was also a grey area of racial mixing.

The effect of apartheid laws was a humiliating and disruptive racial discrimination glossed over as 'differentiation', which purported to be built on the 'separate-but-equal' concept. The fraud was exposed inexorably: the separate facilities for blacks were scandalous. Education, health services, residential areas, transport – everything was woefully inadequate, both in quantity and in quality. Grievances over hardships and indignities sparked off more and more frequent risings.

Under pressure these laws, too, were systematically amended

and relaxed, especially as they had become unenforceable. At the time of publication of this book a few apartheid laws remain in force, notably the Group Areas Act (racially segregated residential areas) and the Population Registration Act (compulsory registration at birth as a member of a racial group). Both in public and in private discussions, however, President De Klerk has committed the government to repealing all apartheid laws. Apart from announcing the scrapping of the Separate Amenities Act, the opening address made it quite clear that no form of racial discrimination would be retained.

The third pillar of apartheid was the concept of racial federation to accommodate the common interests of all racial groups. Although never explicitly mentioned in official documents, this concept eventually crystallized into a policy. Initially it was hoped that the black states would join the whites in a kind of constellation of states. The coloured people and the Indians countrywide would make up their own provinces without borders and would be allowed some form of autonomy in their own affairs as well as a say in the white-controlled state. The same arrangement would apply to blacks in 'white areas'.

Later a different formula was used. Whites, coloured people and Indians entered into a federation, organized in the Tricameral Parliament. Each group was given autonomy in its own affairs, but common affairs were governed jointly by way of committees, consensus procedures and other means of settling disputes. White authority over the other two groups remained entrenched in this arrangement. Granted, it did broaden democracy in a sense; but it nonetheless remained rooted in racial segregation and white domination.

Since the black majorities had been left out in the cold they were offered a sop: a 'black parliament', set up beside the Tricameral Parliament, would consist of the governments of the black states, representatives of black local authorities, and members elected in black elections.

The two parliaments (the mixed Tricameral Parliament and the black one) would be loosely joined in a confederation – this was Plan A. Later another idea was mooted: the three chambers

58

of the present Parliament should integrate into one chamber and a second black chamber should be set up. The two would then form a kind of federation with a joint cabinet and a system of consociation and consensus to prevent domination by either parliament.

In this way apartheid floundered from crisis to crisis with one equally unworkable plan succeeding the other.

In principle, the presidential address of February 2 scrapped these ideas. The aim, one gathers, is to be a Western democracy with a non-racial system of government founded on a common voters' roll. (This would amount to majority government, with built-in safeguards for minorities.)

The fact remains, what made apartheid disintegrate was its seven fallacies.

First, the order apartheid was supposed to create did not materialize. Founded on dreams of mathematical precision and geometrical formulae, it had tried to compartmentalize everything into neat squares, areas and institutions separated by philosophies and laws and administration. This ideal was unattainable because the majority of South Africans rejected it. The revolt against this ideological orderliness took various forms, both domestically and abroad; in consequence, order had to be sustained by force, manifested in the structural violence of a quasi-dictatorship lashing out like an enraged bull. Order was overtaken by chaos because that order was unnatural; it had attempted to subjugate and violate reality – the reality of ordinary people living their lives.

Second, the arithmetic of apartheid was faulty and obtuse. By what reckoning could one syphon off 21 million people in 1980, 37 million in the year 2000, and 48 million in 2010, into 30 per cent of South Africa's land area, leaving the rest of the country for 10 million whites? By what computation would this handful of whites keep hold of their monopoly on power? It began to strike home that, numerically, the whites had been swamped anyway, and that they could best survive by becoming part of the system, part of the majority. Apartheid spelled doom for the whites, for by isolating them it vitiated their influence. Apartheid was steamrollered by the arithmetic of numbers.

Third, the balance sheets put paid to apartheid. Since the astronomical sums of money its enforcement demanded were simply not available, it was financially unworkable. Once the taps of international capital investment and loans had been turned off, apartheid began to stare the spectre of bankruptcy in the face.

Fourth, the immorality of apartheid avenged itself on the system: the immoral basic philosophy that minorities could dominate majorities through a conspiracy of power and discrimination; the immorality of the lie that apartheid merely gave others what one claimed for oneself; the immorality of the arrant hypocrisy that claimed to have designed a system that safeguarded civilized values and represented custodianship over the less privileged. Step by step, these immoralities were exposed as self-assertion and egotism, as self-advancement at the expense of others, as uncharitable and unjust. Although it was not intended or recognized as such, apartheid had been feeding on evil. It was darkness masquerading as light. Since apartheid was essentially criminal, it could not prevail.

Fifth, apartheid was transparently a sophisticated system of racism. Culture was never really at issue; what mattered was the colour of one's skin. White was equated with racial superiority and black with racial inferiority; white was the province of Christian dignity, black the reign of uncivilized inferiority. Since it was fundamentally insulting, apartheid had to be destroyed.

Sixth, apartheid underestimated the forces of black nationalism. An old maxim claimed that as long as a black had a full stomach and a roof over his head, he was the happiest man on earth. This was simply another form of racism: it was a notion that held that blacks lacked the needs of human dignity – pride, affiliation and self-determination. Revolt was dismissed as the product of incitement and communism. Apartheid failed to account for a black nationalism that demanded, uncompromisingly, the right to govern oneself in one's own fatherland. In its thirst for liberty, nationalism showed apartheid the door.

Seventh, apartheid's sheer complicatedness made it suspect.

60

Systems, procedures and structures were evolved from the axiom that South Africa, being a complex country, was the great exception in the world. The architects of apartheid were hoist by their own petard. Those very convolutions betrayed skullduggery; for when clarity goes by the board one need seldom look far for dishonesty.

One question rankles: How could F W de Klerk be party, for more than a decade, to the designing and maintenance of a system founded on evil? Will he outlive that shadow of his past? Can someone with 'the mark of Cain' lead South Africa into a non-apartheid dispensation? Has he not simply made an opportunistic change of garment whilst still harbouring the canker of apartheid in his heart and mind? The question is unfair. Apartheid was a corporate effort by generations of whites, a legacy of Dutch and British colonialism. When apartheid was institutionalized, F W was a boy of twelve, one of a generation that grew up with the concept of apartheid.

But do F W and his government see apartheid as evil, and would they affirm my diagnosis of the seven fallacies of apartheid? Frankly, I am not quite sure. They might well concede that all seven factors had played a role, but they would focus on the impracticality of the system rather than its immorality. Politicians do not readily admit failure; perhaps one should spare them that loss of face. In my opinion, however, it is a great pity that there has been no public and forthright confession that apartheid had been a fallacy. I think F W owes South Africa that confession.

Government spokesmen – including F W de Klerk – often use the following rationalization: The white (Afrikaner) bears no guilt in the sense of deliberate malice and plotting against the blacks. The whites tried to come to an arrangement with non-whites through negotiations and bargaining. There had been mistakes, but generations of whites had worked constructively to further black interests. The policy of separate development was an attempt to affirm liberty, justice, self-expression and self-preservation whilst rejecting domination. It had sought to be a fair and just dispensation.

People will have to jettison this argument. It is untenable, and it contains no more than a modicum of truth.

What is awaited is a confession of guilt: the guilt of wasted opportunities, shortsightedness, and complacency; the guilt of greed, of trying to skim off the cream for the whites; the guilt of allowing segregation to run rampant, until its tendrils had smothered unity to near-extinction; the guilt of alienation, rejection, and arrogance.

Of course blacks, too, have their record of guilt, but at this point in our history it is the whites whose guilt is at issue.

Politicians, as said before, are chary of public penance; yet the question remains whether such a public profession of failure and guilt is not still missing from F W's rhetoric. It might go a long way towards creating a climate for negotiation.

Would such a confession of guilt spark off hatred among blacks? Surprisingly, they still show a remarkable capacity for forgiveness, even after all their sufferings. This is evident from numerous statements by black leaders.

It is an old truism that forgiveness demands confession, and to black leaders it seems as if F W is refusing to make that confession. In an interview one of them told me: 'F W is still radiating paternalism, as if he is doing us a generous favour by even considering granting us a place in the sun.' I do not think F W is radiating that image, but the perception persists in certain quarters.

5

That F W de Klerk may still be harbouring an adapted and camouflaged model of apartheid somewhere at the back of his mind is, of course, suspected in certain quarters. That suspicion is founded on his ultra-conservative image, as discussed earlier, but it is also fed by his harping on group rights, group areas, and a communal lifestyle. Only two years ago it was still clear that 'groups', to him, meant racial groups.

The National Party's stated policy is power-sharing. (In earlier versions of apartheid it was the division of power, with every racial group in charge of its own affairs.) In essence, this seems to imply that white power is to be shared with black power – thus, once again, a matter of racial groups. What else could it mean? And who would be sharing power with whom? It seems that the idea of a federation of races still prevails. The notion of sharing white power and black power runs counter to the concept of a non-racial democracy.

Another question is whether the concepts of white education and non-white education, white land and non-white land, white hospitals and non-white hospitals, 'own affairs' and 'general affairs', and many more, do not imply that the notion of racial groups is still being smuggled in through the back door.

Even the new formulation of minorities – without the group concept – seems to be a euphemism for racial minorities. The new concept of group formation through voluntary association is seen as the scrapping of established racial groups merely to have them re-group along the same racial lines, albeit voluntarily. Until quite recently the plan in National Party circles was to set up a procedure for voluntary registration with the group one chose to identify with, and it is predicted that any such grouping would again be mainly on racial lines.

In an interview the State President told me that he had in recent times often spoken to representatives of various ethnic groups – including blacks – who had voiced concern about their ethnic integrity in a future dispensation. They were concerned not only about their own ethnic culture but also about ethnic participation in decision-making.

F W formulated his perception as follows: 'As long as all non-whites were still united in their rejection of white domination, the ethnic political awareness faded into the background. Now that a new dispensation of non-ethnic politics is in the pipeline, internal differences are beginning to crystallize. It is not my strategy to encourage that process, nor to use it to divide South Africans on ethnic political lines. But what is becoming clear is that the South African realities cannot be ignored. In many countries all over the world, a multi-cultural and multi-national situation is a force to be reckoned with, even as far as race is concerned. I do not believe in the existence of anything like a non-racial society in the literal sense of the word – look at America and England. What we have to build is a non-racist society, in which colour would not be a criterion for political subdivision; but the diversity of our people would not disappear in such a society.'

It is strongly feared that the facts of race and ethnicity will destroy the new South Africa. Multi-ethnicity is a fact, and so is the Afrikaner's historical record on race.

The Afrikaners (and, one should certainly add, the English-speaking South Africans) rigidly preserved the traditional colour bar, elevated discrimination to a right, and paternalistically entrenched the master-servant relationship. Various explanations have been offered for that record: that Calvinism had created a sense of superiority and exclusivity; that the colour bar was drawn by disparities in civilization that were conspicuous until recently, and in some cases still are; that the Afrikaners, fearing the numerical superiority of the blacks, had mobilized themselves as an ethnic minority to gain and retain power; that, since early times, the Afrikaners (as frontier farmers in the old Cape Colony) and the blacks had seen each other as enemies, and that since those times there had always been confrontation and friction.

Historians are unanimous that the two most important principles serving as cornerstones for Afrikaners and validating their national existence were the republican ideal and the theory and practice of inequality between black and white. Thus race and colour became politicized in South Africa, charged with pent-up emotions, and highly flammable. A conflict-free society in South Africa is a pipe-dream.

In the meantime, black racism, too, has gained enormous momentum, even as a world-wide phenomenon. After World War II, it became a tide of opposition against traditional South African politics. It was apartheid that brought the Afrikaners to power in 1948, in a near-desperate attempt to stem the tide of black nationalism. The voters believed that white salvation lay in the beating off of black claims. In the face of the entire world's

64

disapproval the white privileged had to ensure their continued existence.

What cannot be denied is that white fears for the future of South Africa are a powerful motive force in our politics – all political groupings recognize that, from the AWB to the ANC. There are those who are feeding these fears, others who are trying to allay them, and still others who scoff at them.

It might be fruitful to begin by admitting that some white fears are justifiable, and that they come under three headings. At the root of all three kinds lies the fact that a black majority government is unavoidable; the whites cannot prevent it. I say this in cold realism. To keep struggling against it would be irresponsible towards the country, towards the future of the whites, and towards all South Africans.

Against that background, the first white fear is of drastic hardship in the future. There would be chaos, it is feared, and everything would collapse: the economy would bog down in poverty and bankruptcy; the social order would disintegrate into violence, lawlessness, intimidation, murder and mayhem; the political system would be corrupted into a black dictatorship waging a reign of terror; the government, the police, the military and the business world would be riddled with corruption; and in the fury and vengefulness of reverse racism the white, particularly the Afrikaner, would be oppressed and discriminated against in everything affecting his life, his property, his work and his institutions. The whites would be made a spectacle.

This fear is, for the most part, unfounded. There might be isolated cases of such hardships, but African government does not spell barbarism: that has not been the experience of whites in Africa, nor is it in the character of black majorities. This kind of fear is an insult to blacks. We, the whites, have good reason to show more trust.

The second white fear is the more rational fear that the white may lose his influence. He would play second fiddle, stripped of his political power and rights; his privileges, economic power and lifestyle would decline; he would be eliminated from the public service, the police, the defence force; his business would be taken over to some extent; he would be crowded out of his schools and his suburbs. The back-row would become his place, and he would have to snap his fingers very loudly to be seen and heard.

This fear is exaggerated. Some of it may be realized, but certainly not everything. The whites form a very strong pillar in this country, and their input on all levels – their traditions, entrepreneurship, management skills, literacy, political experience and economic ability – is indispensable. They might no longer be the bosses, or even the senior partners, but they would remain partners, and through their contribution they could find a niche in a new South Africa.

The third white fear is fear of Africanization: that the entire South African system would shift from a Western orientation to an African orientation, with human rights and judicial systems, management styles, democracy, economic policy, education, general services, decision-making – everything African.

This is a realistic fear, because our systems will not remain untouched – there will be adjustments and compromises. But does that mean the new South Africa is doomed? By no means. There are encouraging signs that the neo-colonialist notion of guardianship is giving way to partnership. Afrikaners are outgrowing colour-bars. Racial isolation – avoiding contact with blacks – is giving way to racial communication on social, sporting, academic and professional levels. Racial entrenchment – discrimination through legislation – is being rapidly dismantled in all areas. Racial anxiety – a lack of confidence in the possibility of a settlement – is dwindling before a new enthusiasm for co-existence and co-survival. The movement away from racist prejudices and entrenchments, and a sensitivity to justice, equality and reconciliation, are becoming dynamic forces in the political mood of the country.

The key might lie in stripping ethnicity of any political content or divisive force to make it, instead, an ethnicity that allows specific cultures and traditions to co-exist in a broader nationalism as part of a new South African family.

Black groupings neither deny nor underestimate ethnic

66

values. In its final report the Kwa-Natal Indaba – a negotiating process between whites and Zulus in the eighties – agreed that ethnic groups should be included in an upper house of a new state and should have a say in matters directly affecting their groups.

In a document of June 15, 1989, the UNO commission on the protection of minorities made the following recommendations:

Believing that indigenous peoples should be free to manage their own affairs to the greatest possible extent, while enjoying equal rights with other citizens in the political, economic and social life ... the right to preserve their cultural identity and traditions and to pursue their own cultural development ... the assistance for the maintenance of their identity and their development ... the right to manifest, teach, practise and observe their own religious traditions and ceremonies ... the right to develop and promote their own languages, and to use them for administrative, juridical, cultural and other purposes ... the right to maintain and develop their traditional economic structures and ways of life.

In 1988 the ANC published its *Constitutional guidelines for a democratic South Africa,* which included the following clause under the heading *National identity*: 'It shall be state policy to promote the growth of a single national identity and loyalty binding on all South Africans. At the same time the state shall recognise the linguistic and cultural diversity of the people and provide facilities for free linguistic and cultural development.'

In other words, the prospects are not as gloomy as white fears would paint them.

The crux will be the concept of safeguarding minority rights. In the parliamentary opening address the State President instructed the Law Commission to draw up a manifesto 'directed at the balanced protection in a future constitution of the human rights of all our citizens as well as of collective units, associations, minorities and peoples' (*Hansard*, February 2, 1990).

In an interview with me, F W de Klerk commented as follows on this point:

'Safeguards against domination by factions are found in constitutions all over the world, including recognized constitutions such as those of the United States, Belgium, Switzerland and Canada.

67

'I am by no means suggesting that minority rights should include the entrenchment of minority privileges or minority domination over majorities. I am speaking of protecting minorities against the abuse of power by the majority.

'In discussions with Western heads of state I encountered no objections to this concept. It was discussed in detail; in fact, it lies at the centre of the European debate, which is all about protecting the say of small countries against large ones.

'What has made the concept of minority rights suspect is that in the past we definitely used it to signify white rights. We are working on a clean sheet now, and our accent on minority rights is by no means a form of hidden apartheid.'

In this interview it became clear that the real problem was to define minorities. F W formulated the following principles for that definition: 'Minorities must be formed by voluntary association; they must not be racist groupings; and no discriminatory basis must be built into minority rights.'

He maintains that minority safeguards should be entrenched in constitutional structures. Purely as an example, he refers to a bicameral system in which one chamber would be elected by a majority vote and the other made up of representatives of specifically defined interest groups.

Asked whether a right of veto would be retained, he replied, 'A veto system is negative. A basis of consensus is more positive and can work. Before a bill could become law in such a model, there would have to be consensus by the executive authority, the general assembly and the chamber of interests.'

Does this mean two voters' rolls? Not necessarily, says F W. 'A differentiated franchise could include two voters' rolls: one would be a one-man, one-vote roll for the general assembly, the other a representative voters' roll for the chamber of interests. It would be possible to get the same results with one voters' roll.'

He also maintains that the executive authority should not be made up unilaterally by the majority party; there are countries whose constitutions allow members of other parties to hold seats in the cabinet, according to a set formula.

The principle of proportional representation is clearly acceptable, whether as a collection of geographically shared units or party-political shared units. As a kind of random check – to see whether 'minorities' still had racial connotations to him – I asked whether proportional representation did not imply a negligible share for minorities in the new state, against an overwhelming majority. His reply was: 'Interest groups cannot be defined solely on the basis of numbers. The concept of interest groups must be defined in terms of a whole number of factors. This will have to be negotiated.' In other words, he insists: 'The two-chamber model is only one example of how minorities can be protected. It is not necessarily my, or the National Party's, proposal or preference.'

The spectre remains of a numerically inferior white group seeking to retain a substantial say on the strength of their merits and their contribution in South Africa.

The question still stands: Has race really been abandoned as a basis for power-sharing in a new constitution? I am convinced that it has been abandoned in principle and that its unacceptability is recognized, but that the search is going on for definitions of minorities that would include safeguards for whites.

This is understandable, since F W would hardly want to sell out the whites to a system in which their say would be worthless.

Trying to entrench white power at any price would be foolhardy and dangerous. Trying to safeguard white power and white systems is, surely, justified. That could be done through a constitution, a bill of rights, structures of government, economic 'constitutions', and so forth, all of which could be achieved by hard bargaining.

Nor is that kind of bargaining impossible. All black political groupings have signified in various ways that the valuable elements of white systems must be retained, even if in adjusted forms. These might include systems of democracy, free enterprise, the supremacy of law, freedom of association, private ownership, labour ethics, training standards, etc.

The fear that we might get a system of government too far removed from democracy is both well-founded and healthy; that fear should be our motive force in all future negotiations.

Whether black, white or brown, we should be prepared to go to war to retain the fundamental values of democracy. We must get rid of the unfounded and exaggerated fears – they are crippling us; but we must fight relentlessly to eliminate the justified fears. Let it be known to everyone that the whites have a 'bottom-line': democracy.

Finding an acceptable compromise on this point is going to be one of the thorniest problems.

6

Apart from the reaction in the world press, the State President's opening address sparked off intense activity in international politics. The traffic of international communiqués to South Africa became a flood: questions about the implications of the speech or about ambiguities, cordial congratulations, and promises to lift sanctions and break South Africa's isolation.

Some incentives did indeed follow: the capital and loan market eased somewhat, international sporting promoters hinted at new possibilities for touring sides, and consideration was given to relaxing cultural boycotts.

The speech clearly confirmed what the State President had told the international community on his overseas visit a few months earlier. Nobody expected an immediate lifting of sanctions, however; at most, the international community was expected to await further developments with cautious optimism.

The scepticism of world-wide anti-apartheid groups, Mandela's warnings (in a direct response to the speech, and during his overseas visits in June, 1990) that there had so far been nothing but words and intentions, and the initial caution of the Bush administration had an inhibiting effect on the international response.

Despite such negative notes, however, the speech had broken South Africa's three decades of isolation. The international view is well summed up in a report on the UNO fact-finding mission to South Africa early in 1990:

President F W de Klerk is praised by international leaders in the UNO report issued here yesterday.

That praise is contained in diplomatic notes several countries have addressed to UNO to convey their views on events in South Africa to the world organization.

In particular, Britain, the EEC and America have praised steps taken in South Africa under President De Klerk's leadership.

In its diplomatic note, Britain stated that the process now begun in South Africa was irrevocable and would lead to major and irreversible changes.

The British government also stated that the situation in South Africa 'had been transformed radically', owing to President De Klerk's courageous steps. In acknowledgement of the progress made, Britain had lifted its ban on new investments and on the promotion of tourism to South Africa.

In concurrence with other EEC countries, Britain would also no longer discourage cultural, scientific or academic contacts, which in themselves might promote dialogue and the abolition of apartheid.

The EEC, which paid tribute to the roles played by President De Klerk and Mr Nelson Mandela, deputy-president of the ANC, confirmed that it would be prepared to consider a gradual relaxation of sanctions once it had seen further evidence of continuing change.

In its note France also intimated that it would be prepared to consider 'progressive relaxation', depending on the progress made with the process of negotiation.

It is generally considered that the course taken by the government holds true promise of constructive political dialogue. It reflects a significant change over the standpoints of its predecessors. Various steps remain to be taken, however, to create an atmosphere conducive to free political activity. (Translated from *Beeld*, July 17, 1990.)

The State President's visit to countries in Europe and Africa shortly after his speech was clearly a positive step. In an interview with me he offered some insight into events on his tour: 'I am not going to be tricked into listing the heads of state I met in some order of preference or ranking. With some of them I got on remarkably well, but in none of them did I sense any kind of tension. Our discussions were absolutely frank, which gave me an opportunity to spell out my vision for the new South Africa. There were very few critical questions, or rather, trick questions. Every head of state was well informed on our situation, and my arguments on our future dispensation were met with concurrence. I got the impression that they saw South Africa as the economic catalyst of Southern Africa, and that they wanted us to bring about a settlement in the subcontinent that would enable them to form ties on all levels with a stable region. I found it encouraging that they understood what ups and downs lay ahead for us, for in any process of negotiation there are ebbs and flows.'

Enough evidence has come in from abroad to show that Mandela's visit, which followed De Klerk's, did not neutralize the positive effects. Nor, in fact, was Mandela set on vilification. Apart from his enthusiasm in front of public audiences, where he sometimes got carried away by the old ANC rhetoric, informed sources report that he made more positive sounds towards heads of state and official concerns with whom he discussed solutions for South Africa. His insistence on continued sanctions is seen as a lever to be used in future negotiations.

Then came the State President's visit to Washington at the end of September, 1990. In just a few days he was established as a world figure.

The force of his message and the high standard of all his speeches and appearances made a deep impression. Calmly and sensitively, in a friendly but assured manner, he handled interview after interview in a way that captured the imagination of his audience. In South Africa people of all shades of opinion were proud of the way he confidently and comfortably handled every agenda, turning each occasion into a personal triumph. Public reaction in America confirmed that he had made a considerable breakthrough.

Nobody expected his visit would immediately bear fruit, but it almost instantly cleared the troubled air of US-South African relations. President Bush's statement after their working session was very positive, almost emotionally involved, showing convincingly that F W had proved the bona fides of the new politics in South Africa.

President Bush himself struck F W de Klerk as a man of integrity and high moral values. The whole visit – including the reception they received at various institutions and from the public – made a lasting impression on F W and Marike.

1 Frederik Willem de Klerk, one month old, with his parents Jan and Corrie and his brother Willem, before his baptism. Mayfair, Johannesburg, 1936.
2 One year old, with his mother and brother. Mayfair, Johannesburg, 1937.

3 Smiles of achievement. FW and his mother celebrate his first step at the age of 13 months.

4 FW and Willem in the garden of the new family home in Mayfair, Johannesburg, 1937.

5

7

5 Four years old, shortly after the family's move to Primrose, Germiston.
6 The joy of a first tricycle. Brother Willem gives instruction.
7 Primary school-days at Tarlton in the Krugersdorp district.

6

8 FW and Marike met while at university in Potchefstroom.
9 Undergraduate at Potchefstroom University.
10 FW (centre back) with fellow students on the Potchefstroom campus.
11 Students and teachers at Potchefstroom University. FW is on the extreme left of the front row.

10

11

12

13

12 Graduation 1957. FW second from right.
13 FW and his father Jan. The picture was taken after his matriculation.
14 The young couple on the way to their wedding reception in Pretoria.
15 Their wedding day – April 11, 1959. FW and Marike were married by brother Willem, then still a minister of religion.

14

15

16

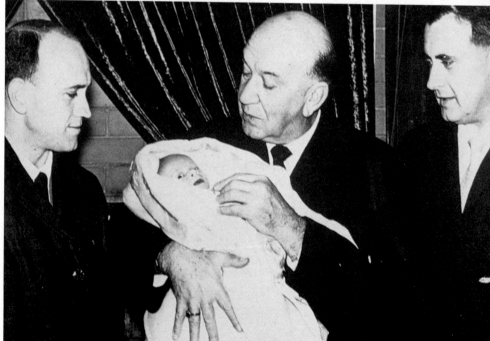

17

16 The proud owner of his first car. FW was then a clerk in a lawyer's office
in Klerksdorp.
17 Three generations of De Klerks at the baptism of FW and Marike's first son, Jan.

18 On September 20, 1989, F W de Klerk was inaugurated as State President.

19

19 State President De Klerk receiving the salute from the State President's guard at the Union Buildings amphitheatre.
20 Taking the Oath of Allegiance at his inauguration.

21

21 The presidential couple after the inauguration with his mother, Mrs Corrie de Klerk (centre),
his brother Dr Willem de Klerk and Dr De Klerk's wife Elzabé.
22 The Parliamentary opening address that changed the course of South African history
– February 2, 1990.
23 A very important handshake in the political history of South Africa – President De Klerk
greets a free Nelson Mandela.

22

23

24 The State President's way of handling the questions of the media with empathy and humour is typical of his new style of leadership.

25 On a visit to the Nancefield hostel in Soweto during September 1990, where he was received with enthusiasm by the residents. (Photo: Robert Botha, *Business Day*.)

26

27

26 With Ruda Landman on the television network M Net.
27 President De Klerk has always found time to keep the media abreast of the latest decisions,
developments and negotiations. (Photo: *The Star.*)

28

29

28 The Groote Schuur Minute –
the first step in the negotiation
process between the government
and the African National
Congress.
29 Relaxing in the Bushveld.

Events would show that this visit was one of the most important missions that F W undertook in 1990.

F W de Klerk, with his speech on February 2, 1990, established himself with the world's leadership as a new, positive force on the Southern African subcontinent. Against the background of our international history, he delivered an unequalled *tour de force*.

7

After the speech the caucus meetings of the parties in the Tricameral Parliament were abuzz. According to National Party spokesmen, their caucus was in a festive mood. The State President was received with tributes and applause. Every member rallied behind him, and there were no discordant notes. The mood was one of jubilation that the National Party had managed to escape from the corner into which it had gradually painted itself.

One of F W de Klerk's greatest achievements is that he has managed to establish a new front of unity in the cabinet and in the caucus. Under P W Botha, tension had sometimes reached breaking point. Although there was almost no open communication, the mood below the surface was one of exhaustion and despair, and gossip and faction-forming were rife. An anti-F W faction tried to persuade P W Botha not to resign, claiming that the National Party would split if F W were to succeed him. In fact, the election for the leadership of the Party showed which way the wind was blowing, for F W was elected by a majority of only eight votes over Barend du Plessis. Yet within a few weeks those same opponents – both in the cabinet and in the caucus – stood solidly and enthusiastically behind F W.

Why? I think there were many reasons, one of them being the fact that any change of leadership brings new spirit. The Conservative Party's recruiting power had grown considerably, and in the face of a common enemy people tend to close ranks, even if they do not always agree. The new challenge of finding solutions to the crises that had developed in South Africa also had a unifying effect.

One of the main factors, however, was F W de Klerk's personality. Not that he was some adored, charismatic figure at whose feet his colleagues huddled – there was too much neutrality about him – but he is a team-man who consults others, takes them into his confidence, honestly shares information with his colleagues, and has a knack for making people feel important and at ease. He is a humane man with a solid sense of courtesy and good manners. Because he is hardly ever aggressive in his style he has made very few enemies. The loyal support he mustered in such a short period was based neither on fear nor on adulation; he had gained the loyalty of trust. His equable temperament, his caution and his rootedness in National Party principles, coupled with natural cordiality, had united people in his support, and once he had set his agenda in motion he began to seize the imagination. His persuasiveness and insight inspired admiration and unity.

I am confident that he will retain his basic humility despite the hallelujah choruses people tend to lavish on men in high positions. Many prominent figures tend to become 'Dada' – the name I use for little idols, for threatening fingers waggled at the world, for smug self-satisfaction, and for dangerous illusions of messianism. In course of time these will feed the lust for power, which is as relentless as any other despot in enforcing its will. I would eat my hat if F W ever became Dada. I will return to the subject of Dada later on.

In any case, he has managed to unite his cabinet and his caucus into a team of inspired colleagues.

According to reports leaked from the caucus of the official opposition – the Conservative Party – the mood after F W's speech was one of fury and dismay. The tenor of most speeches was that De Klerk had finally capitulated, that he had betrayed the country and sold out the whites, and that he had deceived the nation by violating his election mandate. Revolt and rebellion were predicted.

It was reported that the caucus of the Democratic Party – the liberal opposition – were also dismayed after the speech, but their dismay was tinged with excitement and suspicion: excitement, because they recognized the speech as a breakthrough and as a victory for their own policy (which it in fact was); yet suspicious, because they were not sure that the National Party had considered all the consequences of what it was doing. The fear was expressed that it would be a mere gesture, to be retracted step by step in typical National Party fashion. In the caucus it was also cautiously suggested that the Democratic Party's future role might be in jeopardy.

The caucuses of the coloured and Indian parties in Parliament applauded the speech in sincere astonishment.

The no-confidence debate that began immediately afterwards, on February 5, reflected the spirit of the various caucuses: enthusiastic support, scepticism, and naked fury.

8

In ANC ranks, F W de Klerk's speech caused a good deal of confusion.

The ANC had been caught on the wrong foot. They had expected Mandela's release, but not the unbanning of the organization itself. In fact, their planned strategy was to use the released Mandela for a massive campaign to demand the unbanning of the ANC. They were going to accuse the government of making symbolic gestures to win overseas support whilst not having the courage to unban the ANC and compete with it on an equal footing. The Harare document's preconditions for negotiation were going to be the cutting edge of their demands for recognition.

That entire strategy collapsed after February 2. From the ANC's point of view its unbanning was ill-timed, in a sense. Suddenly it had to operate normally. At ground level it was poorly organized. It lacked the infrastructure of branches and management on various levels, and funds were tight. It had not had time to confer – the indaba procedure, whereby joint decisions are taken in council, is traditional to the ANC. Owing to Oliver

Tambo's illness its leadership was vacant. The collapse of communism in Eastern Europe had partly destroyed its power-base and support system abroad; in fact, setting up new relations with East Bloc countries was high on its agenda.

A further source of concern was the tension that flared up occasionally between the leaders of the ANC's internal partners (the UDF and Cosatu) and its own leaders in Lusaka, Zambia. Apart from differences in emphasis, there was also a kind of competition as to who carried most weight in decision-making. The ANC is reluctant to admit that such tensions exist, but there is enough evidence to conclude that friction had occurred from time to time.

The ANC was grappling with the problem of violence, which had assumed critical proportions in the Eastern Cape and in Natal, and the revolt smouldering in black metropolitan townships did in fact later erupt. The young people, caught in a spiral of violent protest, also demanded attention.

February 2 changed the whole scenario for the ANC. From being part of the 'struggle', it had suddenly become part of the 'system'. From being an organized underground army it had been converted overnight into a public political organization. Its communications, which had been confidential within its own circles, now suddenly surfaced in the arena of public accounting and questioning. Where it had basked in foreign applause for its fight against apartheid, the ANC now found itself having to account to its benefactors for its policies and pronouncements. Within a few hours, the ANC was plunged into the democratic political process – and was not quite ready for it. The South African government had snatched the initiative.

The ambivalence of the ANC's initial statements should be seen against this background. They vacillated between violence and non-violence; they declared themselves ready for negotiation, then threatened withdrawal and set new pre-conditions for negotiation; they stood by their policy of nationalizing prominent business sectors and spoke economics like Marxists and socialists, then edged over towards a free market economy; they professed understanding for white fears and for the protection

76

of minority rights, then suddenly declared that the winner would take all in a future South Africa; in commenting on the government and F W de Klerk's intentions they alternated affirmations of trust with loud misgivings and cynicism; conciliatory noises about Buthelezi and Inkatha switched at the drop of a hat to total rejection of any advances.

Caught unprepared on February 2, the ANC created an impression of confusion, disorganization and inertia – a response that caused tremors both locally and abroad. The stock exchange showed itself sensitive to ANC pronouncements; businessmen became more and more sceptical; whites were upset and deserted the National Party because, as they maintained, the ANC had proved itself untrustworthy and was working to a hidden agenda. Abroad, pressure against the ANC mounted, especially because of its statements on economic policy and Mandela's affinity with some arch-enemies of the West such as Gaddafi, Arafat, and the Irish Republican Army.

Fortunately, F W de Klerk kept a cool head. His philosophical remark to me about the ANC's see-sawing was, 'I don't take it too seriously; for a disrupted party, politics is often a matter of casting about to left and right in search of a fruitful middle course. I know many people in my electorate are drifting away because I haven't taken Mandela by the throat, but in these times of reorientation that would simply make matters worse. I shall wait for the ANC at the negotiating table; that will be the time for strong standpoints and for finding consensus.'

I can think of three further reasons for the ANC's apparent unreadiness.

First, they may be using vacillation to preserve their power-base and prevent defection. Once they have built up their infrastructure they will be in a better position to speak out clearly, since they will then have the necessary grassroots communication. They do have a problem with their image: in some quarters it is felt that they have become too moderate, too trusting of government motives, and too humbly grateful for what they receive. The PAC, a more radical black-consciousness movement, is waiting in the wings to strengthen its own position at the expense of the ANC, and there are rumours that Cosatu and other trade union movements are inclined towards more radical rhetoric and action. The rebellious youths remain a problem, since they can be placated and impressed only by shows of aggression. The South African Communist Party is another element that keeps its own options open.

Another problem is that the masses have to be educated to understand the reformulation of ANC policy, after the disintegration of its policy basis before the realities of South Africa and the modern world and the failure of communism. In that process of education a fine balance has to be struck between assurances that the dependable old ANC is still operating, and the justification of adjustments and innovations. If that balance is upset, people will tend to fall back on old certainties and policies. This is why the ANC appears to be playing it both ways.

It should also be added, of course, that it is sound strategy to hold some levers for negotiation. One such lever is to scare your opponents with tough talk, since this might soften them up.

Against this background it is sometimes suggested – or even hoped – that the ANC might split up: since it cannot be all things to all men, it cannot hold irreconcilable elements together. I do not think this will happen too easily. Despite tensions and different emphases, black political solidarity is a passionate cause. It is more likely that power bases will be consolidated now; in two or three years, perhaps, a realignment in ANC ranks may see groups breaking away to more radical fronts.

I am also convinced that the ANC has no dangerous hidden agenda. They certainly have a variety of strategies and options, but they are essentially trustworthy partners in the construction of a new democracy. I have had confidential talks with ANC leaders over a period of years, and I have questioned knowledgeable South Africans who have close ties with the ANC. The overall impression is that the ANC is sincerely committed to the following values: a multi-party, non-racial democracy; the protection of minority rights, provided they carry no taint of racial groupings; an independent judiciary; a mixed economy with strict controls to eliminate the disadvantages of blacks; and

78

a number of other compromises that might be necessary for a meaningful settlement.

The going will not always be smooth, of course – the ANC has a decidedly Marxist basis and African orientation. It does not want to alienate the broad masses, with their excessive expectations. It maintains unambiguously that the will of the majority will have to prevail and that minorities will have to sacrifice more than majorities are prepared to give; it remains suspicious, and is therefore often hypersensitive and stubbornly committed to its standpoints; and it also has an ideological orientation that bogs down in rigidity from time to time, as well as a lack of realism and pragmatism.

Serious criticism could be levelled at the ANC. It has still to prove itself on many points. It continues to make noises about a totalitarian state and has not entirely banished the impression that it has a hidden agenda.

Although the inclusion of the ANC was inevitable, F W de Klerk is also involved in a gamble. If he had wanted to he could have used the fancy footwork of the professional politician to make fewer moves. If P W Botha was credited with the courage to venture into political reform, F W also deserves that honour – he had the courage to leap, and by doing so shook off the image of the man in the middle of the road. He gave a demonstration of strong leadership.

Mandela and De Klerk now carry the keys to the future.

Nelson Mandela and his inner circle deserve all credit for steering the ANC through the difficult period after February 2. He has made some mistakes, of course; but he remains a remarkable man who after 27 years of imprisonment, and with all the ills and ailments of his years, can still provide dynamic leadership. He belongs to the old generation of politicians, and his political style betrays some of that, but he is nevertheless one of the most charismatic South African leaders of the past two decades.

A member of his inner circle, who prides himself on being most critical of Mandela (and therefore prefers to remain anonymous), describes him as follows: 'Mandela's personal style reveals conflicting characteristics. At times he can be very autocratic and unyielding, even on trivialities; at other times he is hesitant and becomes involved in lengthy discussions. But his authority is indisputable. He has a very acute grasp of political issues, and he is a persuasive speaker and tough negotiator. I should call him idealistic rather than pragmatic. He is a very powerful presence, with his dapper figure and elegant suits. As long as he remains alive and well he will be a father figure in the ANC, one we can proudly display on television. Do not misunderstand me – the man is well loved, and a hero.'

It seems as if the two leaders – Mandela and De Klerk – have a lot of mutual respect. Mandela has on numerous occasions referred to F W as a man of integrity, and in a personal conversation with me F W said the following of him: 'He is a man with tremendous style. I believe he is sincerely in search of a peaceful solution. I respect his abilities. He is a politician to be reckoned with. I have no doubt that we will get along well on a give-and-take basis.'

In some respects opposites attract each other. F W and Mandela are opponents on many points of policy, but they are also partners in an unusual alliance: precisely because they are opposing forces, they have to work together to keep the negotiating process on track. They are two poles of the same truth, joined together in an equilibrium of power, compromise, and loyalty to a cause, to maintain a delicate balance over the abyss.

Each has his own individualism. Mandela is more extrovert, F W more introvert. Mandela is emotional and inflammatory, F W persuasive and intellectual. Each has his own dignity, founded on the inherent strength of his personality. Both have an excellent sense of humour and a ready wit – they can think on their feet. Both are men of the smile, although F W has a shy, almost self-effacing smile, and Mandela the broad, self-assured smile of joy. Both have a democratic style of leadership, which is highly regarded in their respective power-bases.

The speech of February 2 left a deep imprint on the ANC – it will never be the same again.

80

The Conservative Party's reactions to the February 2 address brought hatred of F W de Klerk to a head. Over a number of months I had searching discussions with him on this point, and I ended up deeply moved by what he told me.

At heart F W is a phlegmatic man, to some extent even fatalistic. He believes that what he is doing is right and that it is the only way to save South Africa. Since he regards the right-wing reaction as a passing phase born of anxiety and insecurity, he is firmly – almost passionately – convinced that they will eventually flock back to the course he has taken. If he were to be rejected by his own people, the Afrikaners, his conscience would be clear, for he would know that he had tried to steer a course that would ensure their survival too.

Inside the political protagonist of the new South Africa, how-ever, is F W the Afrikaner, and it is this inner core that suffers. In the most profound sense he is driven by his concern for the survival of his own people in their fatherland, seeking a future for them in full nationhood together with others – a future of full opportunities for their Afrikanerdom, in which their language, identity, culture and traditions will flourish.

F W is essentially an Afrikaner with very deep national roots. His family – his great-grandfathers, his grandfathers, his father and his mother – played a leading role in the Afrikaner move-ment. From childhood he was steeped in the significance of Kruger Day and the Covenant (our family regularly attended Afrikaner national festivals), of the 'age of injustice' imposed on the Boers by the English, of the 'black peril', and of loyalty to the Afrikaner nation. Although never ultra-conservative, we were very deeply rooted in Afrikaner values of the Transvaal brand. In terms of our education, betrayal of the Afrikaner cause was tantamount to blasphemy.

Throughout F W's career, a passionate concern for Afrikaner interests has formed a leitmotiv. This is why he is deeply dis-tressed by the curses so many Afrikaners are raining on him. Among his close associates, his amiable smile vanishes when he speaks of the failure of so many of his own people to understand that the new South Africa, which is being wrought with blood and sweat, is a venture for their survival too.

His sentiments may well be shared by all Afrikaners who support the new politics. The role of the Afrikaner's supposed feelings of guilt about apartheid and his sense of justice is much overrated. Even the sober assessment of South African realities is not the primary motive of the 'new Afrikaners'. In the deepest sense, that motive is an attempt to pioneer a course that will secure Afrikaners a future together with other groups in this country. That motive must never be underestimated. Even the right-wing Afrikaner resistance demonstrates – albeit wrong-headedly – the mysticism of Afrikaner nationalism. The 'new Afrikaners' have renounced exclusivism, forever abandoned domination over other groups, buried discrimination, outgrown colour prejudice and racism ... yet they still see themselves as a nation with inalienable rights.

The new political Afrikaner taking shape under the De Klerk regime is indeed threatening the 'old Afrikaners' of the Conservative Party alliance. To understand the dynamics of South Africa one has to understand the anatomy of the conservative political grouping. Their fundamental philosophy or ideology has four roots.

The first is the distorted religious conviction that the Afrikaners are a type of Old Testament Israel, a chosen people with a very special mission, and are therefore predestined to a separate existence.

The second is a concept of racial exclusivity that demands the preservation of a white identity and rejects any form of miscegenation, so much so that racial mixing is regarded as a violation of the laws of nature. The Afrikaner nation is seen as the inner core of that white identity, but other whites are welcome to associate themselves with it.

The third pillar is the premise that a permanent solution can be found only in apartheid or partition, and that this is the only way to resolve all conflict in South Africa.

The fourth is the moral justification of racial exclusivity by claiming that self-preservation is one of the highest values, even if it involves discriminating against other groups. Nationalism demands exclusion and isolation; one has to define the boundaries of one's own group and concentrate on consolidating the power of that group.

The Conservative Party, then, is not simply a political party; it is a highly charged ideological movement that stresses exclusivism, intolerance and absolutism, all under the mystical cloak of a divine mission. It follows a rigid policy of racial segregation in all social spheres: in religion, culture, politics, social intercourse and education – both biologically and territorially.

The party's non-negotiable political principles are the following: the country must be partitioned off into national states to ensure that each racial group has its own fatherland – a white-coloured-Indian state, and various states for black peoples; each fatherland must be governed by sovereign authorities elected exclusively by the citizens of that fatherland; since power-sharing in any form is a violation of group sovereignty, no more than collaborative pacts should be concluded between the various states; blacks and other coloured people within the white state should receive a form of local autonomy in their own townships. This partitioning must be negotiated, enshrined in legislation, and, if need be, enforced by the security forces.

F W de Klerk's accession to office has had three major implications for the Conservative Party.

They are faced with a choice of strategies. The first question is whether or not they are going to take part in the proposed negotiations. If they did take part, they would have to decide which model of partitioning they wanted to espouse – the Verwoerdian model, which claimed 80 per cent of the country for the whites; the secessionary model, which would imply a national state in a smaller area; a white province within a federal, mixed South Africa; or, from their point of view, the least attractive option of entrenched white minority rights in a black majority state.

Is partitioning a totally absurd policy? In itself it is no 'sin'; all over the world there are social groups, especially minority ones, that propagate separation and independence from the majority groups. If I had to play the devil's advocate I might even make out an argument for partitioning as a last resort.

Let us suppose all negotiation, compromise and reconciliation had failed; that power-sharing had foundered on irreconcilable conflict and civil war; that the new politics had gone up in flames and we found ourselves trapped in a destructive stalemate; and let us suppose all these things happened over a decade or so. Some form of partitioning could then be an alternative option. It would, however, have to be a mutually agreed partitioning, a kind of cease-fire, which would also need international recognition. Partitioning could not be imposed through the barrel of a gun; to stand any chance of succeeding, it would have to be founded on a settlement.

Let me make myself quite clear: I am not advocating partitioning. I do not believe it would be in the interests of the whites.

I must assume that my white compatriots who have opted for partitioning have not done so lightly. But they should also appreciate that there is strong resentment of the way they are propagating that option. To allay those misgivings they would have to strip their option of four dubious accretions:

They would have to strip it of emotional bravado. The pious indignation with which they dump it on the table is in itself offensive to others.

They would have to strip it of greed. The claim that everything except the national states and independent states belongs to the whites (read Afrikaners) betrays an intolerable degree of cupidity.

They would have to strip it of racism and chauvinism. Their obsession with colour, their exclusivism, their affectation of a divine mission, and their self-aggrandisement are so transparent that their claims lose all legitimacy.

They would have to strip it of inflammatory protest. People are being swept along on a wave of hysteria and irrational manipulation, and utopian propaganda is disseminated recklessly.

If the partitionists really wanted to take an eschatological line they should rather give the Afrikaner an honest vision of the three horses of the Apocalypse that might sweep over us: the crimson horse of the sword, the black horse of hardship, and the pale horse of sudden disaster. Let them spell out the price of partitioning.

If any group wanted to advocate partitioning they should do so more intellectually, positively, and worthily. Why not begin with a declaration of intent? They might adopt the following line: we are entering a new era in South African history, one in which reconciliation is being sought in the midst of polarization and confrontation; we offer the hand of reconciliation and call down the curtain over the mutual misunderstandings of the past; we believe that partitioning can offer a fair and just solution to South African political problems; partitionists are prepared to rethink the division of land to take account of the demographic realities of our country and to provide viable space where all might grow and prosper; the various models and consequences of partitioning will be subjected to incisive scientific examination; we shall strive for consensus on partitioning in the process of negotiation; we welcome the politics of peace that has become the order of the day; and we should like to defend our option through democratic bargaining around the negotiating table.

A second consequence of the De Klerk policy is that the Conservative Party has stepped up the pace of ethnic mobilization. It is building up a complex infrastructure in all spheres of Afrikaner society – in party politics, cultural organizations, churches, local governments, and a range of social institutions. Where it cannot gain control through infiltration it sets up alternative structures: 'Aksie Toekomsgesprek' has become its Broederbond; the Volkswag is an alternative to the Federation of Afrikaans Cultural Associations (the FAK); and the Afrikaans Protestant Church has become a substitute for the Dutch Reformed Church. On other levels the party is striking up alliances with sympathetic organizations such as the Afrikaner Weerstandsbeweging and a multitude of other radical white factions.

That this mobilization of Afrikaners has certainly syphoned

off support from F W de Klerk and the National Party is reflected in an opinion poll of May, 1990, which showed that only 27 per cent of the whites believed De Klerk was leading the country in the right direction. It is estimated – also after a by-election in Umlazi, Natal – that the Conservative Party now represents more than 40 per cent of the white electorate. The by-election in Randburg suggested a flattening-off of support, but in this case there were special circumstances. The Conservative Party is more and more successfully setting itself up as the symbol of Afrikaner nationalism, whereas to many Afrikaners the National Party has assumed the image of a weakling bowing down to the 'enemy' and throwing in the towel.

F W de Klerk foresaw this development, and it speaks volumes for his courage and conviction that he has taken the risk of alienating his strongest power-base, the Afrikaners. The prime quality of his leadership is that he is doing what he believes is right. This is not arrogance; it is self-confidence and a firm commitment to principles.

Despite its intensified mobilization, however, the Conservative Party is also having problems with the consolidation of its power-base: its unity is being subverted by internal friction about policy options, divergent styles, and jealousies.

A third effect of the De Klerk regime on the right wing is a strong tendency towards revolutionary violence. White armed violence is virtually a foregone conclusion because the right wing know that they will not get their own way at the negotiating table. Assaults on blacks, bombs at National Party offices, the stockpiling of weapons, and assassination threats against De Klerk and his colleagues are the order of the day.

It is clear that all these activities are aimed at derailing the process of negotiation. Set on upholding white domination, the right wing has endorsed the strategy of armed resistance, should it become necessary.

In an interview with *Beeld*, published on July 16, 1990, Minister Stoffel van der Merwe remarked that the growing violence among ultra-rightwing elements in the country was 'basically the same kind of thing' as the leftist and black violence of the fifties and sixties, but that there was less justification for right-wing violence.

Dr Van der Merwe accused the Conservative Party of fostering right-wing violence – even if not directly – with its claim that the government lacked a mandate for its reform measures. This was formerly also the slogan of black radicals. As with black violence then, the motivation for ultra-rightwing violence has a strong racist element. In the fifties and sixties the leftist slogan was 'Black is beautiful'; now the ultra-rightwing says, 'White is right'.

The reasons leftist blacks then gave and ultra-rightwing whites are now giving for violence as a means to achieving their ends are the same. Blacks then claimed that the government did not represent them, that the government was acting without a mandate, and that they saw no hope along constitutional channels. 'That is basically what the right wing is now propagating,' Dr Van der Merwe said. 'They should reflect on the fact that they are now doing what the leftist blacks were then doing. The only difference is that there is less justification for their actions now than the blacks then had for theirs.' Dr Van der Merwe said one of his reasons for saying this was that, unlike the blacks at the time, all white South Africans had the vote.

Leftist violence initially took the same form as the present ultra-rightwing violence, namely sabotage such as bomb attacks on party offices and other centres.

As internal dissent among leftist groups – including the ANC and the PAC – had then made it difficult to build up a power-base, ultra-rightwing groups might now face the same difficulties, Dr Van der Merwe said. Such tensions were not inevitable, but he would not be surprised if they did surface; in fact, there had already been signs of internecine strife in ultra-rightwing circles.

He said it was hard to predict how widespread right-wing violence might become; one could but hope that it would not become too serious. On methods of stopping right-wing violence, Dr Van der Merwe remarked that moral and philosophical persuasion should be backed up by firm police action against perpetrators. The government, he said, should emphasize the democratic process, constantly pointing out that it did have a mandate for its actions and that there was thus no justification for violence. 'That is what we told the leftists at the time, and that is what we now have to tell the right wing,' Dr Van der Merwe said.

In South Africa it is commonly feared that the Conservative Party might take over the government in a white election. That would herald a doomsday scenario, since it would lead to the final confrontation, to a massive revolution, and to total international isolation. The country would grind to a halt like a city under siege, and everybody would begin toppling pillars in a final paroxysm of self-destruction.

Could the Conservative Party and its associates destroy everything that F W de Klerk stands for? I do not believe it will happen.

This vision is the typical response of people who feel threatened because they see themselves as driven into a suicidal corner. It is an exaggerated scenario, created in an attempt to inhibit the new politics and used as a form of intimidation by people who know that they have been virtually eliminated from the political process. Of the future total voting public of South Africa they represent barely four per cent. It is unlikely that another white election will be held, but there may well be a referendum on the principles of a new constitution. Even if the white votes in the referendum were counted separately, one can safely predict that the majority of the whites would vote Yes.

I also believe that a fair measure of success with the negotiating process and progress towards allaying white fears would bring many of these people to their senses, since they would come to realize that the Conservative Party's policy is untenable and impracticable. A new national culture is developing, one that seems to be moving away from the narrow, ethnically defined concept of Afrikanerdom to a broader, unifying nationalism.

F W de Klerk stands a very good chance not only of overcoming the Afrikaner resistance against him but also of

88

mobilizing an even stronger body of Afrikaners behind him.

10

Within the liberal white opposition – the Democratic Party – the initiatives of the De Klerk government also upset the applecart.

This party, which represents some 25 per cent of the white vote, was born in April, 1989, of a merger of factions to the left of the National Party. Its appeal was vested in a number of policies: its policy of a non-racial democracy that rejected racial groupings as the elements of a new constitution; its insistence on a bill of rights for South Africa; its policy of giving priority to negotiations that would include the ANC; its policy that drastic measures were needed to correct the economic disadvantages of the blacks; its policy of free association in the formation of political parties; a common voters' roll; and the total abolition of apartheid.

The Democratic Party could claim that it was a builder of bridges towards the ANC and other extra-parliamentary black groups – a role built up painstakingly over many years – and could therefore act as an honest broker in the negotiating process. Unlike the National Party, which seemed to be powerless in this arena, the Democratic Party could get negotiations going and, by doing so, help to break South Africa's international isolation.

This reads exactly like the National Party programme under F W de Klerk. Moreover it took the National Party only a few months to put into action just about everything the Democratic Party had projected for the future.

The Democratic Party suddenly found itself in limbo, its policy highjacked and put into practice by the National Party. Reports from all over the country suggest that the Democratic Party has foundered on irrelevance. One of its three leaders, Wynand Malan, has resigned, and discussions in the party's inner echelons suggest that its decline is irreversible. Various strategies are being considered: the Democratic Party can dissolve and merge either with the National Party or with the ANC, as individual members prefer; another option is to remain a watchdog for liberal political values, a pressure group that would act as the conscience of both the National Party and the ANC in the negotiating process. If the National Party slipped up and made a mess of the new politics, the Democratic Party could keep the ball rolling.

I know that the founding of the Democratic Party had paved the way for the National Party's rapid shift – a proposition I shall argue in the next chapter – but here the simple fact may be stated that one man, F W de Klerk, has managed, with a few deft moves, to highjack a white opposition party and give it the *coup de grâce*.

11

The speech on February 2 sparked off further eruptions of violence in Natal.

One direct cause of that violence is the battle for support – and for a power-base at the negotiating table – between Inkatha and the ANC: Mandela and Buthelezi are squaring up to each other. But this is not the sole cause of violence in South Africa; its roots lie much deeper.

At the risk of sounding flippant or callous, I must state that war and violence will always be with us. They run in our blood, in the very air we breathe. At no point in our history have we been free of them, nor shall we ever be. South Africa, too, is a land of violence. We shall simply have to live with that.

No one can point a finger, for since the earliest history of our country blood has flowed on all sides: violence of blacks against blacks, in which vast numbers died; white violence, in which blacks were massacred; blacks making every effort to exterminate whites; and whites rebelling against whites. This is the gory thread that runs through our history. All groups have been quick to adopt violence as a solution – not only the Boers and the blacks; for of the English, too, it is written, 'Enter the British … motivated by imperialism, deceit, greed, prejudice … the colony's new rulers would play a leading role in constructing one

90

of the world's most troubled societies.' (*Illustrated History of South Africa*, p. 94; The Reader's Digest, 1988.)

And so it has been to this day. In recent years, and again in recent months, we have time and again seen the ebb and flow of violence in burning townships, in corpses in the streets, in gangs committing murder, robbery and destruction, in civil war among black factions, in whites organizing themselves for revenge against blacks, in pick handles, pangas, guns, Casspirs. Violence comes and goes, but we know it is always lurking somewhere around the corner.

Ours is a violent country. It is nonsense to claim that apartheid is to blame for all violence, and it is utopian folly to think that we shall escape violence in the transition to post-apartheid and the new dispensation. As violence is a universal element in the behaviour of mankind and nations, so it is part of our national tradition – typical colonialistic violence, violent resistance against conquerors, and faction violence in tribal wars.

Ours is a country of many nationalisms, cultures, and social systems, and economically we are divided into rich and poor. Sharp polarization keeps the option of violence alive in South Africa, for that polarization has developed into confrontation on all levels. The ANC, having adopted violence as a political strategy, has demonstrated that strategy over the years; and the government, in turn, has used the 'total onslaught' as a strategy to justify plunging us into an endless cycle of war and mobilization. For long periods, schools were used as the frontline of terror and sabotage, and grievances on any matter under the sun were literally blazoned abroad with death and arson. Incitement, wrath, revenge and protest have become a breeding ground for violence against whites; and fears of mass revolution and of a loss of control have driven the white regime to a camouflaged form of violent oppression.

Violence is also an offshoot of the tyranny of radicalism, absolutism and ideology that seems to be plaguing our continent. Liberation by violence has become an African way of life, spurred on by the sanguinary philosophies of a century in which politics and crime have joined forces under spurious banners.

These were the philosophies that were, so to speak, legitimized by people like Jean-Paul Sartre, of whom Paul Johnson wrote, 'It was Sartre who invented the verbal technique of identifying the existing order as "violent" ... thus justifying killing to overthrow it. He asserted: For me the essential problem is to reject the theory according to which the left ought not to answer violence with violence.' (Paul Johnson, 1988: *The Intellectuals*.)

Furthermore, world history shows that throughout the centuries violence has accompanied transitional politics. As soon as repressive measures are relaxed and political and social reforms get under way, the masses react with more demands and with extortion through an escalation of unrest coupled to lawlessness, provocation, crime and killing.

Against that background, and in all realism, we have to accept the fact of violence in our country. It will be sporadic, sometimes more extensive and more intense, sometimes with phases of cooling, and will, one hopes, be phased out as we progress towards a settlement in our country. Much of apartheid remains to be cleared up, and as long as its detritus lies scattered over the land people will use it as a pretext for advocating the option of violence.

I am not trying to justify violence; I am merely trying to understand it. Law and order must be maintained with a firm hand, and no less firmly must we pursue negotiation as means towards a solution. Black leaders carry the responsibility of enlightening their people and establishing a network of civilized disciplines. The political ethos of non-violence must be promoted in all spheres.

Violence will not disappear overnight. Distressing though it may be, we shall have to temper our distress with realism.

12

If, then, all the political parties in South Africa reached a turning-point on February 2, in what direction are they going to turn?

The State President commented as follows on this question:

'Forming alliances between political parties is a sound strategy. Its advantage is that one develops a new entity – the alliance – which leaves room for differences and special identities as well as agreement and unity on certain issues. But alliances must be managed correctly, and the timing must be right; for if one forms alliances with minor factions one might alienate the mainstream of political thought.'

My own point of view can be summed up in a well-known saying by Dr D F Malan: 'Bring together what belongs together by inner conviction.' The State President recently cited those words as a political ideal for our country; the point is, however, that it now means something totally different from what it meant in Malan's time.

It cannot mean that the Afrikaners should (or could) be reunited politically. The political schism between the Conservative Party alliance and the National Party is too fundamental, their political philosophies too irreconcilable. Let us hope many Afrikaners will eventually come out of the bolt-hole of an Afrikaner homeland to help face the new national task confronting us.

Nor can it mean whites should be brought together; for such a mustering of whites would be as futile as it is confrontational.

If it means that the blacks and the whites, as two political factions, must strike some accord on common interests, it can mean no more than an interim phase. As long as we keep thinking in black and white terms, we shall remain racists – we are then still counting heads by the colour of people's skins, and that means we would have to count about ten black heads for every white one.

In present-day South Africa, bringing together what belongs together by inner conviction can mean only this: that people (not races, nor ethnic groups) who support the same political philosophy should grow together into one political grouping. The course to take would be the formation of new political parties, made up non-racially on the basis of each party's specific policies.

Apart from its contribution to the new political society, such a development would also be good arithmetic. Let us consider the numerical implications. Suppose the totally unthinkable came to pass and all white voters joined the same party. Even now they make up an insignificant percentage of the total electorate (and that percentage is declining by the year). If all the coloured people and the Asians also joined that party, the joint non-black vote would make up barely a third of the total. Add all the KwaZulu voters, and that party would still have a minority vote in South Africa. (The notion that all would be well if only the Boers and the Zulus could come to terms, is rubbish.)

It would be realistic to conclude that any party relying on a single race or on an ethnic conglomeration of non-blacks would be a non-starter in the race for power, quite apart from the fact that racial parties are unacceptable to the majority of South Africans. Culturally, ethnicity will always be a living force, but as a primary instrument of political power it is as dead as the dodo. The National Party seems to have become more and more aware of that fact. If the government were to cling to that notion (which is unthinkable), the National Party would have no influence and no impact on future politics. As far as a partnership in future politics is concerned, the Conservative Party has already disqualified itself.

We must have non-racial and non-ethnic political parties, which will have to canvas the entire population for support for their specific programmes. By this means one will be joining together what belongs together by inner political conviction.

It is conceivable that two large centrist parties might then develop, with two smaller radical parties left and right of the centre. Party A might draw together all who believed in a form of Western democracy and a free market economy, whereas Party B might accommodate more authoritarian, socialistic sentiments.

The centrist parties ought to be fairly well matched. It is becoming more and more clear, for example, that a strong faction in the ANC is leaning towards the basic pattern of a Western democracy. The further negotiation progresses, especially in 1991, the more will blacks be faced with clear political options.

After initial black solidarity, differences may crystallize out more clearly and decisively over a number of years.

The question is whether the National Party should open its door to become a non-racial centrist Party A.

F W de Klerk took the first step in that direction with his speech before the Natal National Party congress on August 31, 1990. Here is the full text of his speech *(translated)*:

Both in 1987 and in 1989 the National Party received a clear mandate to negotiate on a new constitution. That mandate included recognition of the right of all South Africans to participate in government on all levels by way of power-sharing without domination.

Power-sharing necessarily includes joint decision-making on matters of common interest in joint constitutional structures.

The rejection of domination implies sharing power in such a manner that no majority will hold absolute power, nor will it be able to abuse its power to prejudice or oppress minorities.

There is a growing realization among all population groups that this new policy offers the only practicable framework for a stable new South Africa. From that realization has grown a need to co-operate, which is emerging more and more clearly from numerous discussions with political and community leaders.

There are several well-founded reasons for that need, including the following: corresponding convictions on important premises and values; the urge to find, through peaceful co-operation, a just and lasting solution for our country's complex problems; a desire to remove the obstructions that are still preventing our country from realizing its full potential for economic growth; and agreement that certain policies and ideologies must be rejected as both dangerous and impracticable.

To put it more simply: the new South Africa demands that those who belong together by inner conviction should come together.

Against that background, the question of political co-operation across the boundaries of existing parties has become highly topical. The concepts of partnership, alliances and open membership are cropping up frequently and spontaneously.

The National Party accepts the fact that in the new South Africa it is helping to build, there will necessarily be rearrangements in the sphere of party politics. The National Party believes, furthermore, that the foundations for future co-operation must be laid now, lest valuable opportunities be lost.

In this regard the party leadership has formulated a number of propositions which are to be submitted to the four Provincial Congresses for ratification:

1. The National Party will strive to bring about alliances or a broad political

movement that would unite those who pursue the same goals on the basis of shared convictions on important principles and values.

2. The existing restrictions on membership of the National Party are in conflict with the Party's declared stand against racial discrimination and are an obstacle to alliances.

   Consequently, Congress now authorizes the National Executive/National Council to effect, after consultation with the Federal Council, the necessary constitutional and procedural amendments with a view to making membership of the National Party accessible to all South Africans.

3. Active competition for membership between parties co-operating as allies is not advisable. Consequently, it is deemed preferable that participating parties should reach accord in this regard.

4. In terms of the mandate it has received, the National Party will continue to pursue the interests and rights of all communities as well as the values it stands for, and to have these confirmed in a new constitution.

If these propositions are ratified by the Congresses, the Federal Council will request that each of the four Provinces nominate an equal number of representatives to a committee entrusted with the task of –

a. drafting, within the framework of the Five-year Action Plan of 1989, a manifesto to serve as the basis for negotiation with a view to forming alliances and/or the founding of a broad political movement, and, in the process, of consulting with individuals or spokesmen of existing parties that are prepared to co-operate in this regard;

b. making recommendations on the question whether within alliances or a broad political movement allowance should be made for individual membership and/or participation by organizations other than political parties;

c. deliberating on the National Party's role in the constitutional process of negotiation, as distinct from the Government's, with due regard for the role of alliances or a new broad political movement, and of making recommendations on this matter;

d. advising on more detailed constitutional proposals;

e. reporting as soon as possible to the Federal Council.

As in negotiations, this course, too, will have its phases. In the first phase, white and black power groupings would negotiate for their mutual accommodation in political structures and decision-making processes. A next phase would be alliance politics. As the DTA initially did in Namibia, political parties with roughly the same policies would form a bloc against other parties. From that phase, it is hoped, would grow a consolidation joining together all adherents of a specific political policy.

Such a development offers the best protection for minority groups. By becoming a political force within the majority, the minority group retains its influence, its say and its impact. If a party paints itself into an exclusive corner, its influence in a democracy is gauged by its numbers; for whites that would mean isolation.

13

The parliamentary opening address of February 2, 1990, undoubtedly marked a turning-point for the political system of South Africa, for our international relations, for the ANC, for the end of apartheid, for the Conservative Party, for the Democratic Party, and also for the National Party.

The eruption of violence has in fact made the country less stable, but it is to be hoped that this is no more than a transitional phase.

The central figure in that turning-point was the State President, F W de Klerk. Through that role alone, he has carved himself a niche in South African history.

3

THE PIONEERS

1

What F W de Klerk did before and after February 2, 1990, had long been in preparation. He ventured a leap, but it was not a leap from zero to ten: a number of strides had already been taken along the way.

The brief history of that leap – the considerations that had led F W and the government since his accession to office – has been considered from various angles. The main forces behind it may be summed up as follows:

Important shifts in international politics, reflected in US-Soviet talks, were improving the climate for world peace. F W's visits abroad before February 2, 1990, showed that the world was more than ready for peace and compromise in South Africa. The government was encouraged by this readiness to support new initiatives. In African politics the winds of change were also blowing strongly: Namibia gained independence and many fears were allayed by its promising start. The civil wars in Angola and Mozambique were starting to move towards peace initiatives and the government promoted better relationships with neighbouring black states as they reached out for South African aid.

The government realized that 1990 was the time to break through the increasing and threatening international isolation. When communism in Eastern Europe dramatically collapsed in one state after another it provided the perfect (and equally dramatic) springboard for the removal of the restrictions on

South African organizations. The support of Eastern European states for the ANC and its affiliates was weakened, which lessened the risk of unbanning these organizations while providing a handy propaganda weapon against socialism. In addition, internal revolt against the apartheid regime was taking on unmanageable proportions.

The union of the European Community in 1992 made it imperative for South Africa to prepare a place for itself in the new European market.

International political movements were a dynamic force behind the move of February 2, 1990. Internally, too, warning lights were flashing. The impracticability, unacceptability and unaffordability of apartheid meant that the whole system was falling apart. The economy was eroded by economic and financial isolation within a fluctuating international economy. The facts of urbanization, demography and escalating demands for social expenditure were inescapable. South Africa had to turn over a new leaf if it was to be able to exploit international economic resources.

The National Party was obliged to make a concrete move towards power-sharing: developments in opposition politics provided the writing on the wall, making action absolutely necessary. The black revolt was becoming uncontrollable and the Conservative Party and Democratic Party had started to erode the National Party's power-base. The new leader, F W de Klerk, had himself grown in clarity and motivation for a breakthrough: it started in 1986 and his first speech as National Party leader on February 8, 1989, gave it expression.

All these elements created the climate for F W's leap. Politicians, as we all know, are highly sensitive to the political climate; only rarely in history has a country's political leadership flown in the face of the prevailing political climate. In that sense politicians are followers rather than leaders. They do not create new ideas; instead, they formulate the public opinion of the day. While flying kites to test the wind, they are under pressure from behind to take the lead in a specific direction.

In political circles that role is summed up in two maxims: keep your ear to the ground, and watch your timing for any political move. Of the first, Winston Churchill remarked, 'People would find it very hard to look up to leaders detected in that somewhat ungainly posture.' And that being so, a good politician needs yet another quality in times of change and crisis: the courage and faith to stand up boldly, to renounce his own interests, and to stake his own reputation. In doing so, he may become the seed that falls to ensure a future harvest.

F W de Klerk has demonstrated what I might sum up as three qualities: the knack of reading the political climate correctly, the ability to time far-reaching announcements, and the clear vision and stamina needed to take a decision and strike out on a new course.

From discussions with F W it is quite clear that he has these qualities. He insists that he is simply implementing the consequences of National Party policy. After the decision to share power with the blacks had been taken and tested in an election during P W Botha's reign, De Klerk had to spell out the consequences of the decision in his government's policy. The time was ripe. He sees himself as a relay runner who, having taken over the baton, now has to run his own lap on the way to the finishing-line. He denies the allegation that his policy reflects discontinuity in National Party policy and, in doing so, admits that the way had been prepared for him, that the climate was right, and that doing what he did had to come almost automatically. Here one catches a glimpse of National Party loyalty – he would be most reluctant to admit that the party had reached an impasse. But one also senses a touch of the politician's anxiety: he wants to make it quite clear that he is still on course, for if the perception is formed that he has deviated from the right track, the climate might turn against him.

In fact, he recognizes the new political climate, which he calls the 'pressure for renewal'. On further questioning it becomes clear that what he has in mind is the need, among all South Africans, for a breakthrough towards solutions. There was a mood of exhaustion, of scepticism, of a despondent impression that we were doomed to stalemates. According to F W, the need for some form of success is a crucial element of the political climate. He has read that climate correctly.

Having done so, he showed the vision of a statesman in taking action and striking out on a new course that has brought positive as well as negative changes to the political climate. It brought hope on all fronts – hope for our international relations, and hope for a settlement through negotiation. On the other hand it also brought panic, because the stability of the country was threatened by mass black action and by the aggressive mobilization of white right-wing movements. In Afrikaner circles, the climate began to turn more and more strongly against F W.

Undeterred, he pressed on to show his stamina as a leader. His own calm has done much to bring calm in public opinion. In an interview with me he commented as follows on this feature of the reaction to his speech: 'I was, of course, disappointed with the instability that flared up everywhere after my opening address. It made me realize once again that political change is a slow process, and that a long road of political re-education lies ahead for all South Africans. But I did not feel threatened. I had expected outbursts of fury and obstructionist tactics in right-wing circles, and the struggle between Inkatha and the ANC had to come to a head some time or other. It's a great pity, however, that it has developed so violently. I can truly say that these reactions did not make me the slightest bit nervous. I had the inner conviction that the time was ripe, more than ripe, for my moves. Things will settle down. In politics, too, one learns to wait. Only calm action will promote the right climate.'

Thus F W was not merely an interpreter but also a creator of the political climate. Instead of simply pursuing the course set by his forerunners, he had set a new course.

2

Various pioneers had created the right political climate for F W de Klerk. I doubt whether National Party spokesmen will ever admit it, but the fact remains that the old Progressive Federal Party, and especially its successor, the Democratic Party, as well as Hendrickse's Labour Party and Buthelezi's Inkatha, had made substantial contributions to the leap of February 2, 1990.

One of the ground rules of politics is that you should appear to be pro-active rather than reactive; you dismiss the opposition as irrelevant and claim full credit for every innovation in your policy, as if it has sprung from inner conviction. This the National Party could hardly claim with a clear conscience. In fact, F W de Klerk's policy looks only too much like a highjacking of opposition politics.

Those 'leftist' political parties had been insisting more and more forcefully on liberal political values and had relentlessly attacked the National Party, clearly setting out the alternative of a non-racial democracy as the only option that could save South Africa from total collapse, and repeatedly exposing the unworkability of government ideology. Although never really a threat in elections, they had functioned as the government's conscience by charging and condemning, by identifying with the cause of the disenfranchised black masses, and by unmasking discrimination with deadly accuracy.

Under the National Party South Africa had in effect developed into a one-party state which had succeeded largely in eroding the power-base of the white liberal opposition. The party had gained wide support among English-speaking voters and influential businessmen.

Denigrated as 'selling out the whites' and as 'collaborating with the total onslaught against our country', the liberal opposition found itself caught between the two poles of white interests and sentiments, on the one hand, and black extra-parliamentary resistance to the government, on the other. In my view they succeeded admirably in balancing these two forces by advocating, on both fronts, the values of Western democracy as a solution for South Africa. Theirs was a lonely and thankless task, performed with great dignity.

For the National Party the founding of the Democratic Party early in 1989 was undoubtedly an unsettling development. It consolidated the Progressive Federal Party, Dr Denis Worrall's Independent Party and Wynand Malan's National Democratic

Movement into a unit that presented a much stronger front than the fragmented leftist opposition of the past. What caused apprehension in the National Party was the interest shown in the Democratic Party by the so-called 'fourth power' – the enlightened Afrikaners. There had been widespread speculation and ample signs that enlightened Afrikaners had had more than enough of the old National Party's stagnation in the last years of the P W Botha regime. Moreover, it was feared that large numbers of English-speakers might desert the National Party, because the Democratic Party was much more acceptable to them than the equally hidebound old Progressive Federal Party.

I want to give special emphasis to the fact that Afrikaner opposition on the left was increasing and that this was confirmed by empirical research. As early as 1984, the Institute for Sociological and Demographic Research of the HSRC, in a country-wide survey, found a high awareness and questioning of the slow pace of reform among 26 per cent of Afrikaners. In 1989 Mark- en Meningsopnames found, also in a country-wide survey, that 48 per cent of Afrikaans-speaking people were in favour of negotiation with the ANC and 42 per cent for the release of Nelson Mandela. I myself surveyed 350 Afrikaners who could be described as enlightened, with a National Party orientation, and 89 per cent broadly agreed on the need to move away from racial groupings as the basis for classification of political power. This 'left wing' within the National Party was a potential market for the Democratic Party.

My own role in the founding of the Democratic Party – as chairman of the talks on the merger and as a candidate for the party's leadership – was deeply disturbing to F W. We had some heated words, followed by penetrating critical discussions on the political policies of the National Party and the Democratic Party. Throughout those discussions – from November, 1988, to September, 1989 – F W maintained that he found the Democratic Party's policy unacceptable. He had strong reservations especially on the party's attitude to the entrenchment of group rights (which he then still saw as the rights of racial groups). Nevertheless, I got the impression that he was showing a new sensibility to the fact that the National Party's policy had reached a dead end and that the Democratic Party was offering a clearcut policy option with distinct possibilities. The road he has followed, step by step, since 1986 has gone in this direction.

Another remarkable reaction on F W's part – and one that reveals much of his integrity and insight – was his sympathetic response to my motivation for breaking away from P W Botha's National Party. As he put it, he appreciated that my choice had been consistent with my enlightened politics. He was never harsh in his reproaches, nor did he strain relations between us. In fact, he was as cordial and relaxed as ever towards me. F W is truly a generous and warmhearted man.

Moreover, he never put any pressure on me to withdraw from the Democratic Party. When I withdrew I did so on my own initiative, for reasons such as the following: I was not interested in an active, full-time political career – a sentiment and point of view I had maintained throughout my public career; I wanted to preserve my independence, credibility and standing as a political consultant and commentator; and I was not prepared to let matters deteriorate into a circus, with two brothers fighting each other on political platforms. Besides, I had gained new hope when F W was elected leader of the National Party, because I had faith in his attitude and in his ability to face reality and pull South African politics out of the doldrums.

In any event, an influential group of Afrikaners had begun to turn against the National Party's policy of a federation of four race groups. Although the Democratic Party did not come up to expectations in the 1989 election, it did draw about 25 per cent of the white vote. Behind closed doors, I happen to know, the National Party noted that the Democratic Party's policy had considerable marketing value.

Furthermore, the Democratic Party had to its credit that it enjoyed access to and was already involved in extensive unofficial negotiations with the black extra-parliamentary groups. It was also stated publicly that they, without the involvement of the government, were going to set up a negotiating table and that the ANC and Inkatha would participate. This, too, made the

104

government apprehensive that the initiative might slip from its hands.

It cannot be denied that the left, through the Democratic Party and its sympathizers, prepared a way for the National Party. The best proof of this is that F W de Klerk has taken over the broad framework of the DP's policy.

There were further developments on the left. Briefly: the unofficial alliance between the National Party and the coloured Labour Party in the Tricameral Parliament went sour, *inter alia* as a result of unedifying clashes between P W Botha and Allan Hendrickse; tension between Buthelezi and the government reached breaking point and co-operation with other homeland leaders wore thin because they began to show more and more affinity with the ANC; and the extra-parliamentary United Democratic Front, the Mass Democratic Movement and the Cosatu trade union alliance set up dangerous barriers of resistance through boycotts and strikes.

The disruptive strategy of the opposition on the left made its mark; for the government, it was the writing on the wall, a warning that it could not continue with its policy.

The power of the pen, too, had its impact. Publications from the left of the government flooded the market, with scenarios which, like Clem Sunter's 'high road and low road', more and more painted the government into a corner. Symposium after symposium was widely reported in the press. The message was that South Africa had finally reached the crossroads.

Sharp attacks came from academics and academic institutions, professional institutes and influential organizations such as Dr Van Zyl Slabbert's IDASA (Institute for a Democratic Alternative for South Africa), to name but one example.

The preparation of the way on the left was carried entirely by the English-language press, who through the years had made a major contribution to political change. In the early sixties and earlier, when the Afrikaans newspapers were conspicuously and exclusively oriented to Afrikaans interests, Afrikaner politics and National Party policy, the English-language press reflected the existence of a total South African society. The existence, problems, aspirations and frustrations of the black and brown communities received constant attention, and South Africa was fully informed that these communities were a political factor that had to be accommodated. By communicating black and brown demands and representing their interests, the English-language press sensitized South Africa to the need for change.

By communicating black views it made South Africa aware of the real opposition in our politics. Its emphasis on black poverty, inadequate housing, blatantly discriminatory legislation and practices, on the rise of black nationalism, and on growing polarization prepared the ground for the politics of change, which is aimed at promoting a racial settlement that would be acceptable also to black and brown.

By stressing the economic fallacies of certain facets of the policy of separate development the English-language press promoted the broadening of policy.

In the face of narrowing influences, the English press aggressively chose the theme of Western traditions to confront the public and its leaders with the political philosophy of freedom and justice, which in turn created the climate for resistance against closed systems.

One should not underestimate the role these English newspapers played in persuading their Afrikaans colleagues to put journalistic freedom above servility. As a background force, their example encouraged the political emancipation of the Afrikaans newspaper.

Although the English-language press had little or no effect on government decisions it was an effective instrument for change because it forcefully presented the 'other side'.

One could well say that leftist opposition factions paved the way for F W de Klerk. Their clout was not in their voting power but in the logical force of their argument that a non-racial democracy was the only solution for South Africa.

3

It may sound odd, even ironic, but I am convinced that the

founding of the Conservative Party also contributed towards the De Klerk leap of February 2, 1990.

Before the split in the National Party, F W worked tirelessly to reconcile the warring factions, so much so that enlightened colleagues began to query his inclinations. In retrospect he had the following to say about those times: 'I had always striven for Afrikaner unity, because I believed it was in the best interests of our people. At times of large political shifts, especially, a united front gives you bargaining power. I believed I could convince the dissidents with reasonable arguments. At no time, however, did I offer them compromises. I insisted that they conform to National Party policy. In the course of my conciliatory efforts, however, it became increasingly clear to me that we were dealing with a break in principle, and that those people's leaders were filled with passionate aggression. I was shocked to realize that they wanted to destroy everything the National Party had built up laboriously over the years. I then turned my back on them and fought them with intense conviction.'

And so he did. In an editorial of April 1, 1982, the morning newspaper *Die Transvaler* wrote *(translated)*:

The outcome of the first full parliamentary confrontation between the National Party and the Conservative Party was predictable – Dr A P Treurnicht has lost yet another round. By contrast, the leader of the National Party in the Transvaal, Minister F W de Klerk, made a strong impression with his frankness and directness.

Minister De Klerk's assessment of the Conservative Party and its leader amounted to the following:

They are pursuing ideological politics designed to lull people; emotional politics to incite people; woolly politics that takes refuge in vagueness; ambivalent see-saw politics, and dishonest politics that tries to charge the National Party with falsehoods and to cover up their own role in the disruption and confusion in the National Party.

As long as they fail to spell out a concrete policy, and as long as they lack the courage to admit to their philosophy of domination, they will have to carry the label of schismatics who have been caught out and are now waging petty politics that doesn't care a rap for solving the country's problems.

I have studied F W's speeches on the Conservative Party in and outside Parliament in the years between 1982 and 1987. I would sum up his judgements as follows:

The Conservative Party is a conglomerate of reactionaries from all quarters, who are reactionary for diverse reasons: they are the embittered and the disaffected in politics; people who are against P W Botha 'on principle'; militant rebels such as the Afrikaner Weerstandsbeweging; Kappie Kommando demonstrators; HNP sympathizers feeding on political negativism; and finally a group of Nationalists who have long been known to see apartheid as absolute segregation on all levels. For them, the great political issues are how to 'purge' post offices, shops, streets and parks of all blacks. And siding with them are a handful of English racists.

The Conservative Party is supported by a remarkable hotchpotch of voters. Such a public usually shows much emotion and enthusiasm, for agitation is the food they live on. They are more against than for: against the National Party and its leadership, but not so much for the truly incisive political planning, vision and policies that can offer solutions. They are a protest group and a pressure group.

The Conservative Party differs in one prime respect from the National Party, and that is that the National Party sees the salvation of the Afrikaner and of all the people in our country in a national settlement, whereas the Conservative Party seeks salvation in the ideological phantom of the Afrikaner's exclusive rights and dominance in the government of our country.

The Conservative Party has ideals, philosophies and ideologies, but with no practicality, realism, clarity or truth. They are utopian propagandists trying to pass off the unworkable for the attainable.

The opposition to them is, therefore, founded on morality: they are misleading the people, because they ignore facts and realities. That deception is an opiate for people who are nervous about the future. In the name of truth we set up political barricades against them, even if they are of our flesh and blood.

That was the tenor of F W's statements on the Conservative Party in the eighties, and those perceptions prepared the ground

108

for F W in the sense that they made him so much riper for the antithesis. In the process of accounting for his philosophical opposition to them, he gained more clarity in his own mind.

This is exactly what happened to Afrikaners outside the Conservative Party: it held up a mirror to them, in which they saw a nightmare, the chimera of dangerous fanaticism, offensive racism, and folly hiding behind piety. They saw their own subconscious, and they began to distance themselves from it, fearful of the dark forces called up by the ideology of apartheid. It had a cathartic effect, compelling them to seek a corrective and to try, pro-actively, to project a different Afrikaner. That mirror drove them to lucidity.

In that sense, then, the Conservative Party helped to pave the way for the new politics.

4

Another forerunner was the enlightened movement among Afrikaners. It merits extensive historical study, for it was a continuous force that developed step by step in the context of cause and effect. Time and again something in the National Party's formulation and implementation of policy elicited reaction, and that reaction grew from cautious questioning to protest through the media. After conflict with the National Party the reaction would gain some ground, and that was usually followed by a gradual policy shift in the enlightened direction. Then came the next round.

Thus, step by step, the enlightened force gained impetus to lead F W de Klerk to February 2, 1990.

There are differences of opinion about the extent of the influence of the enlightened movement among Afrikaners on the course of South African politics. Generally speaking, it was certainly not the primary force, but F W would never have been able to risk his quantum leap had enlightened politics not prepared the way for his initiatives. Therefore it was an important factor and deserves attention. As far as I know, no publication, to date, gives a perspective on the enlightened movement.

I am not going to discuss the enlightened movement in historical terms; instead, I shall draw on my own experiences, participation and assessments. I should like to consider the movement's role in the identification of ultra-conservatism; the method of incremental renewal; the course of the enlightened debate; and the unstructured nature of that action.

One force-field of Afrikaner enlightenment was the identification, definition and confrontation, and finally the exclusion of the ultra-conservatives from the mainstream of Afrikaner political thinking. I coined the term *'verkrampte* Afrikaner' – for ultra-conservatives – in a speech before a youth congress at Warmbad in 1966, when I outlined the following basic characteristics of that *verkrampte*: 'His watchword is: back to the old ways. He stands for the continuation of the past; closing his mind to innovation, he casts suspicion on anyone and anything that advocates openness to criticism. He lives and thinks by a system of regulations that have gained validity over the years, without questioning the principles of those regulations. He is trapped in political stagnation. He is a propagandist for the bigoted, traditionalistic, isolated Afrikaner, ever ready to launch a campaign against heresy, and skilled in the extremistic use of hairsplitting to enforce his views on any issue.'

The speech strongly suggested that certain aspects of the apartheid policy should be thrown open for review. From the media there was positive support for the view that ultra-conservatism was poison, but at the same time some prominent Afrikaner cultural leaders protested vehemently that a wedge was being driven between Afrikaners.

The concept of *verkramptheid* then became established as uncritical support for the apartheid policy, whereas *verlig* (enlightened) became a cliché to describe Afrikaners who were seeking renewal and change in political policies. The informal political grouping within the National Party began to take shape around these two terms. The first official split came in 1969, when the Herstigte Nasionale Party broke away from Prime Minister John Vorster's National Party and political ultra-con-

110

servatism became defined as a political party. At the same time, however, a significant number of ultra-conservatives stayed on in the National Party. Heated debates were waged in the media, but spokesmen for enlightenment were few and far between because the dominant spirit in the National Party was ultra-conservative. Prime Minister John Vorster hovered between the two factions but tended to lapse every so often into ultra-conservatism. Gradually, however, and inch by inch, the enlightened faction began to make headway by pressing for policy changes on certain points.

At the time the debate centred especially on the so-called 'opening up' of facilities. Vorster's government began to relax apartheid by opening facilities such as hotels and theatres to non-whites. Sporting policy, too, began edging towards mixed teams.

At the time, as stated earlier, F W de Klerk held consistently to the interpretation of official policy, although he tended to put stronger emphasis on the ultra-conservative pole. The enlightened faction, at least, saw F W as an ultra-conservative sympathizer, and the conservatives were only too keen to claim him for their faction whenever it suited them. In his own view he was a man in the middle of the road.

The most aggressive ultra-conservative strategist was Dr Andries Treurnicht, whose ambiguous pronouncements kept his cause in public view. Step by step, however, the enlightened faction flushed him from his bolt-holes, thus preparing the ground for his faction's break with the National Party in 1982. I should like to recount just one anecdote to illustrate how the enlightened faction handled that exposure. In *Die Transvaler* of November 19, 1976, a cartoon was drawn of Treurnicht back to front on horseback, and pulling the horse's tail to slow it down. It caused quite a stir, not least in government circles, and Prime Minister John Vorster challenged me to account for it.

I should like to quote *(translated)* portions of my letter to him to illustrate how the enlightened faction identified ultra-conservatism.

My dear Mr Vorster,

I appreciate your frankly disapproving response to *Die Transvaler's* editorial and cartoon of Friday, November 19, 1976.

The crux of your objection – and I hope I read it correctly – is the following:

That Dr Treurnicht is being accused of overt or covert suspicion-mongering or subversion of the development of the policy. And that he is disloyal.

Your direct question to me demands, in effect, that I produce proof for these statements, since to your knowledge Dr Treurnicht's pronouncements and interpretations of policy are fully in line with those of the National Party.

Before dealing with the 'proof' – I shall prefer to put it differently at a later stage – I should first like to account for the editorial and the cartoon.

1. The context and tenor of the editorial are that all kinds of conspiracies should not be sought behind Dr Treurnicht – he is a spokesman for a faction within the National Party whose rigid view of apartheid regards racially mixed situations as a move towards integration.

The line continues through the proposition that the spirit of the National Party's development of policy is taking a different course. And that there must be sensitivity to that course, that 'spirit' of further development.

If people seem to be arousing a feeling against it – as Dr Treurnicht may be seen to be doing – it amounts to subversion, suspicion-mongering and disloyalty. The cartoon tries to express this point: one should not try to force the horse backwards.

If that is not how it was interpreted, then I am sorry. I deliberately did not want to attack Dr Treurnicht; I wanted to present him as an example of a certain attitude.

The crucial thought was that people should not undermine the spirit of the 'new road the National Party is breaking open for its policy'.

2. I have many grounds for the statement that a certain faction in the National Party is casting suspicion on the development of policy. Here are some of them:

– the many letters and responses received by *Die Transvaler* that accuse the National Party of deviation, integration and selling out.

– Reactions perceived when I address or attend gatherings of bodies such as the Rapportryers and other groups.

– Personal conversations.

– Certain MPs' views as expressed in conversations.

At this time any pronouncements that create the impression that the National Party is balking and dragging its feet are especially dangerous to it. They confuse people and sow suspicion. They stimulate doubt and uncertainty.

They contribute towards creating a split image for the National Party, and a crisis of credibility.

They entrench two 'warring factions' within the National Party, which is not conducive towards the National Party's great task.

112

3. Dr Treurnicht is one of the people who tend to create that impression.

The point at issue is the *one-sidedness* of his statements, at least in many cases. The *carelessness* of his formulations. Thus he contributes towards subversion and suspicion-mongering.

I may mention some examples:

a) About April, 1973, Dr Treurnicht showed a tendency in the House of Assembly to present white domination, apartheid and discrimination as resistance to renewal and the further development of policy.

b) Dr Treurnicht on discrimination in *Die Transvaler* of February 4, 1975:

'For that reason there are homelands, group areas and white areas. Against that background, and on that basis, I simply cannot see how one could apply a policy of no discrimination.

'For if you were to do that, you would be prejudicing the freedom of the white. No discrimination would mean, *inter alia*, that we would have to have open membership in all sports clubs, societies and organizations, but this is essentially in conflict with the policy or philosophy of the separate development of peoples. Anyone who would indiscriminately consider all people of the same country, regardless of colour or national affiliation, for posts in the public service, sport, church life, and so forth, has no leg to stand on in relation to political apartheid.'

c) Dr Treurnicht on sport, *Rapport*, July 18, 1976:

'You would be creating a different social structure if you extended mixed sport from the invitation teams, which are made up for special occasions, to a regular phenomenon on provincial and club level.

'I do not think that is the intention. If it were, then it would mean integration in sport.

'I should therefore like to say this: we must be careful not to begin, at a given point in our social structure, a process of breaking open that could penetrate to other facets of our social life.'

d) Dr Treurnicht on theatres, *Rapport*, June 6, 1976:

'The decision to open the Nico Malan Theatre to mixed audiences was pushed through in a way that creates many problems for the government's decision to be consistent in such matters.'

The fact that mixed gatherings are the exception is National Party policy. But he keeps harping *one-sidedly* on that theme, whilst saying as little as possible about the positive side of opening up. And that smacks of subversion.

For example, again in *Beeld* of November 13, 1976:

'The opening of theatre, church and other facilities to all population groups simply does not tally with the government's policy of separate development.

'By opening such facilities one cannot build separate communities.

'How can one build structures of separate political freedom on a distintegrated social life?'

e) Dr Treurnicht on international hotels, *Rapport*, June 6, 1976:

'Hotels are different and are used for transient traffic. In any case, it is only for foreign blacks.

'If it is the case – as at Jan Smuts Airport – that blacks go there only for meals or for drinks, then the situation is being abused.

'The facilities (hotels) are not available to ordinary workers.'

These are only a few examples. His statements immediately before Soweto could also be cited.

His statements in public, and in private (which I have personally heard or which have been recounted to me), tend to be one-sided. And there is consensus on that in broad circles.

It is a question of nuances and accents that reflect a narrower and more exclusive accent in colour relations than that emanating from the National Party, and in particular from you.

In that sense it is undermining, complicating, retarding and confusing National Party policy.

You are no doubt aware that nearly all Afrikaans newspapers, numerous Nationalists, many MPs – also from the North – have the same opinion of Dr Treurnicht.

The image he is projecting is that he is riding the horse back to front.

I hope that, after this memo, you will also understand the motives for the stand I have taken.

It was an attempt to defend the credibility of the National Party's policy development. And to voice disapproval of pronouncements that might create the impression of disloyalty to the spirit of the new policy development.

These identification tactics were applied on numerous fronts. The two accents within the National Party were repeatedly highlighted, because the enlightened faction refused to cover up the fact that the National Party was sitting on two chairs. It goes without saying that this enlightened outspokenness created much tension in the system. Vorster was furious, and enlightened people repeatedly had to put up with humiliating insults, also from his ministers.

Under the P W Botha regime the internal conflict came to a head. Dr Treurnicht and 21 MPs protested against the concept of power-sharing between whites, coloured people and Indians. When everybody tried to be conciliatory, the enlightened Afrikaner movement pressed openly for schism and expulsion. I should like to quote an article in *Die Transvaler* of February 24, 1982, as an example of the move for expulsion *(translated)*:

The Cabinet convened on Monday for a special meeting after serious tension had arisen in National Party circles around the concept of power-sharing.

That report brought points of disagreement into the open. Other disagreements, however, are being kept from the public eye.

We are being confronted more and more with the question whether these differences in the National Party are growth-pains or the pains of disease.

If they are growth-pains they are positive things. They then represent a search for clarity, a process of weighing the pros and cons, and standpoints that rub against each other in order to find consensus in the process of decision-making.

If they are the pains of disease they are something negative. They are then faction-forming and the confrontation of different philosophies consolidating their own power-bases while moving away from each other.

With growth-pains one should exercise patience, tolerance and accommodation.

The pains of disease, however, call for a different treatment. Their intensity and magnitude must be determined, and then one of four decisions must be taken:

Must the problem be allowed to suppurate until the body has been purified? Or should one intervene, even with an amputation? Or should one simply live with it, hoping that the body is strong enough to drag along the ailing leg? Or should soft hands keep rubbing in soothing ointment?

Our view, in brief, is the following:

We have always regarded the tensions in the National Party as growth-pains, with now and then an infection.

Keeping the team talking, and keeping them together, has borne fruit.

More and more, however, we are beginning to fear that many of the consensus moves are made under a kind of compulsion. Silence for the sake of peace, before the common threat, in one's own interests, to wait and see, or whatever.

True consensus clears up a dispute, but if the old contentions are repeatedly resurrected, so to speak, we do not trust that consensus.

Now, again, the Prime Minister has said about his statement on one country and one government for whites, coloured people and Indians: 'Every minister is expected to abide by the statement.' And there is clearly a buzzing among one or two ministers and their sympathizers, who appear to be abiding by it but in private and in small groups are putting down a *No* foot.

To an informed observer, then, the consensus on crucial matters looks rather shaky.

How deep-seated are these disagreements? On certain matters they are accents and disagreements on methods – certainly. But differences in principle also seem to be increasing, although many are still hidden. Among MPs only a very small group seem to be crossing swords with the present line of policy, but among National Party voters the crossing of swords seems to be more widespread.

Political unity in the Afrikaner corps also seems to be rather shaky. Since that is so, any future decisions will have to be highly responsible.

Where the pains of disease are becoming noticeable it is definitely time to start counting the risks. Gentle, soothing hands make for stinking wounds. The result may be serious infection of the National Party body.

Connivance with that treatment may lead to paralysis. Many have spotted that tendency towards paralysis.

The moment of decision on the philosophical options will have to come. Whites, coloured people and Indians form one state, share one citizenship in one fatherland governed by one government. This does not mean power-sharing in a unitary state, but rather that structures are being created for joint deliberation and decision-making on all three tiers of government, without endangering self-determination.

The other option is three states with their own territories dispersed like a patchwork quilt, with three governments deliberating and co-operating in a loose form of consultation, as in a confederation, but still with the white Parliament as the supreme authority.

There are various accents and formulations, but ultimately these are the two options. We cannot put off making our choice.

When the die was cast shortly after this article and the split became a reality it signalled a major victory for the enlightened movement. The front page leader in *Die Transvaler* of March 1, 1982, commented as follows *(translated)*:

The representative Transvaal executive of the National Party has voted overwhelmingly and unambiguously for the policy as it is developing under Mr P W Botha.

It is no doubt well known that *Die Transvaler* – against much opposition – has been advocating and debating that development of policy for the past eight years. Consequently it is a very special day for us now that those who resisted it have been defeated.

We strongly hope that the period given for reflection until Wednesday will make many dissidents see the light.

Those who are not prepared to do so can in no way expect the support of this newspaper under its present leadership. We support the official policy of the Transvaal National Party.

The Transvaal ministers concerned deserve congratulations for their handling of the whole matter. According to reports, Minister F W de Klerk must be congratulated on his positive guidance.

That applies equally to the vast majority of the MPs and MPCs and the representatives of divisional committees who exercised their sound judgement in the honest process of evaluation.

116

It is to be expected that the battle to influence voters in the various constituencies towards one side or the other will grow very heated. We hope that here, too, the strategy will be not half-heartedness and cover-ups but frank statements in keeping with the lead given by the national executive; so that the National Party's unity of policy may continue to be promoted and this whole incident may become nothing but a breakaway of a splinter group.

Transvaal Nationalists may rest assured that the realistic and evolutionary application of the basic principles of the National Party is in sound hands.

All that has happened is that the National Party has honestly admitted that co-responsibility necessitates a form of healthy power-sharing with the retention of self-determination. Only along that way can the National Party remain in power as a party that guarantees a future dispensation of just co-existence and neighbourliness.

To return to F W de Klerk: in this process, in which the enlightened Afrikaners identified, defined, confronted, isolated and expelled the ultra-conservatives, he, too, went through a phase of development.

I would describe those phases as follows: initially the perception existed that he sympathized with the ultra-conservative camp (which he denies, but which was seen as such); then followed his cautious phase, in which he tried, like so many of us, to steer a middle course that put equal stress on the two facets of National Party policy, the ultra-conservative and the enlightened, with a tendency (again a perception, not an admission on his part) to lean towards ultra-conservatism; then followed his phase as a peace-maker trying to prevent a split; following that came his outspoken phase as an acute and deadly adversary of the ultra-conservatives; and finally, round about February 2, 1990, came the phase of his final choice of enlightened politics.

In his own mind the expulsion of the ultra-conservatives over the years had prepared the way for his choices, but it also prepared the way for a 'purified' National Party that was ripe for risking the leap with him.

5

In retrospect, the method of the enlightened Afrikaner movement may be described as follows: it was a movement of incremental political renewal which tried, inch by inch and in tiny doses, to shift the government and the Afrikaner nation from the accent of segregation and apartheid to the accent of unity.

At the same time it was characterized by caution and a kind of conservatism, since it kept on clinging to the concept of separate development. It took the view that it would be politically, psychologically and educationally responsible to influence people gradually, to plant one little seed after another and wait for each little crop before sowing the next batch. With each new step ahead, assurances were given that the advantages and disadvantages were put on the scales, and through creative repetition over many months people were persuaded that the advantages of renewal and change were greater and safer than clinging to the old policies.

The belief persisted that this is the only effective method of moving people – and specifically Afrikaners – without precipitating dramatic resistance, which would set back the whole process considerably. There is yet another danger, and that is that Afrikaners are quick to excommunicate. In the political process of breaking away from apartheid some influential Afrikaners fell by the wayside because they had come out too suddenly and too uncompromisingly. Afrikaners have an absolutist streak that works on the antithesis of friend and foe. They are suspicious of the grey area of healthy relativism and critical enquiry.

A further feature of the Afrikaners is their 'messianic' and 'eternalistic' perspective. They feel secure as long as only one way, one truth and one life are presented to them as the ultimate answer, and they seek reassurance and safeguards for the most distant future and for their furthest descendants. In politics they do not hold with the maxim that fortune favours the bold.

Against that background, in the opinion of the enlightened faction, the rule of thumb is that he who wishes to be an agent for change must keep one foot in the Afrikaner establishment and must make reassuring noises while the ground is shifting.

The question arises whether the enlightened faction's strategy

118

of eye-dropper renewal was a form of dishonesty. Were they not deceiving people with dribs and drabs of change that in themselves seemed fairly innocuous but in fact carried the germ of further and further advances, until there could be no turning back? Did the enlightened movement keep quiet about the consequences of those gradual changes?

The answer is yes and no. Critics of the enlightened movement may justly claim that the changes were too well sugared with the assurance that separate development would not go by the board. But the concealment was not intentional; the enlightened faction believed that they might be able to salvage some of the principles of the old policy, if only the corrections and the promotion of unity could progress more rapidly. This was in fact held against them by the so-called *oorverligte* (ultra-enlightened) Afrikaners.

Further criticism was that the enlightened Afrikaners were not dynamic or aggressive enough in promoting their views. They were too placatory, too ready to withdraw into weak moderation when confronted with opposition.

I would admit, then, that the enlightened movement did not pave the way for a radical break with separate development. It was only a good deal later – towards the end of 1988 – that it made its great leap towards acceptance of the fact that a black majority government was inevitable and need not spell disaster. That leap was precipitated by P W Botha's fall.

At that stage F W had not yet accepted this point of view, but he was on the threshold of a breakthrough. In a discussion he intimated that he realized that power should be shared with blacks, but that black majorities should certainly be presented with the counterpole, namely joint decision-making by, and the safeguarding of, minorities.

The gradual promotion of enlightened politics between 1973 and 1986 made Afrikaner attitudes ripe for the De Klerk era.

The force at work among Afrikaners of the eighties must be read correctly.

It was the evolution of the Afrikaners as a nation in transition towards a new identity.

The evolution from the isolation of self-aggrandisement to the realization that Afrikaners cannot walk the road alone.

The evolution of being prepared to make themselves acceptable to black Africa and the West by moving away from racism and shedding ethnicity towards identifying themselves with a co-existence in which segregation is not the dominant factor.

The evolution from infantile insecurity to self-assurance on a more positive and mature level.

The evolution from accepting the apartheid system in all its details, to its critical examination.

The evolution from self-exculpation to a salutory awareness of national guilt.

The evolution from ideological politics to realistic politics.

The accent was moving from exclusivity to inclusivity, from centripetal energy to the centrifugal energy of common interests, from separation to cohesion, from apartheid to shared interests.

The motive for the evolution was anxiety about survival, but it was also a new vision of himself, of concepts such as democracy, justice and equality.

That evolution was not mere rhetoric and symbolic gestures or cosmetics. It was a ground movement shifting some towards a new philosophy while others were still running away from the breakthrough, and yet others caught in the dilemma of doubt.

That evolution was tentatively beginning to seek a change in political policies that might bring about a national settlement in South Africa.

During the late eighties the National Party Afrikaners pushed through that evolution in their readiness to accept F W de Klerk's policy and to give it their enthusiastic support.

6

Over the years, the enlightened debate introduced new seminal concepts into politics and paved the way for their acceptance and incorporation in official policy changes by the National

Party. Step by step, enlightenment amongst Afrikaners gained a kind of respectability in the National Party, whereas ultra-conservatism was more and more seen as disreputable.

The seminal concept in enlightened thinking was communality, the counterpole to segregation. This concept was developed in various ways and its consequences were drawn through to all levels of society. It was argued that the National Party had bogged down in segregation, which had become an over-developed feature of its policy. It had minimalized communality and had become counter-productive. Segregation had frustrated and crowded out communality.

Taking its stand on the realities of South Africa, the enlightened movement began to attack apartheid on its seven fallacies (see Chapter 2): that the order apartheid had sought to impose had failed; that apartheid was doomed by arithmetic; that the financial balance sheets had proved apartheid unaffordable; that the immorality of the policy had to be acknowledged; that racism lay at the root of apartheid; that black peoples had justified nationalistic claims; and that the complications of the system were proof of its impracticability.

Communality, it was argued, held the key to solutions, and this was spelled out with a series of new concepts in the National Party's vocabulary.

The bonds of a common destiny were emphasized by pointing out that black and white were interdependent and intertwined, and that the whites, specifically the Afrikaners, could not make it alone. The egotism of domination and survivalism would boomerang.

Co-existence, too, was a new concept, set up beside the survivalism that had long motivated National Party thinking. A feature of co-existence that gained ground was the concept of sound neighbourly relations between ethnic groups. Co-existence sought to account for the fact that we are an integrated society and that this should be expressed in all spheres.

In different phases of political development, the enlightened movement put varying accents on co-existence. First they spoke of consultation; then of association; then of consociation or power-sharing between white, coloured and Indian and a con-federal association with black states; then of a federation of racial groups; then of a federation of various territorial units; and finally of a non-racial unitary state. With these concepts the enlightened movement was always a jump ahead of the National Party, but policy shifts followed the enlightened lead.

The enlightened movement advocated constitutional co-exis-tence, arguing that the existing constitution offered no model for a settlement; co-responsibility of all groups had to be built into a constitution. This was developed step by step into joint decision-making, equal participation, power-sharing, and a democratic dispensation that recognized the majority principle and demanded the protection of minorities.

Enlightenment came out more and more strongly against racial grouping as a principle of a new constitution – against strong resistance on the part of the National Party.

Social co-existence imposes demands that were strongly argued by the enlightened movement. Among the new concepts harped on relentlessly were closer communication between the groups; the abolition of the so-called 'petty apartheid' that sought to isolate races in their own areas; sharing facilities; and the grey area of racial mixing, which was projected as normal in the South African situation.

Economic co-existence was a pet theme of the enlightened movement, with the emphasis on the blacks' valid grievances about housing, wages, transport, training, labour, education, and so forth, which had reduced them to a poverty culture and had exacerbated their disadvantages in the inequitable apart-heid system.

In a strong appeal for juridical co-existence, enlightenment came out time and again against the network of discriminatory laws. As the political process of phasing out discrimination prog-ressed, these laws were laid on the table one by one. Justice and equality became the watchwords, and any chance was seized on to confront the authorities with them. The principles of a con-stitutional state were propagated and the government was persistently and sharply confronted with the question of security legislation and its application.

Religious co-existence was advocated, with accents on the untenability of racial segregation in church communities; protest against the exclusion of black and brown Christians; objections to the separation between the mother church (white) and daughter churches (black and brown); questions about the Church's sanctioning of the apartheid policy; and an appeal to the Church to counter racial alienation with reconciliation.

In numerous other issues the enlightened movement was a forerunner and a watchdog. It fought courageously for the freedom of the press; for the relaxation of ultra-conservative censorship systems; against the perils of a camouflaged dictatorship; for the necessity of a Bill of Rights; for the promotion of negotiating processes that could succeed only if they were founded on willingness to compromise; for the unbanning of the ANC and recognition of the fact that the ANC was the leading actor in black politics; to expose the war-cry of the 'total onslaught' as a propagandistic exaggeration; and to sensitize the authorities and the public to the urgency of our situation and the need for a rapid, planned tempo of change.

7

The enlightened movement among Afrikaners was not an organized, structured campaign. There was no caucusing behind closed doors, no orchestrated strategy. Leading figures emerged, but there was never a leader, a committee, or a co-ordinator. The reason is obvious: the enlightened faction formed part of the National Party and exerted pressure from within, each in his own way and manner. Until the Democratic Party was founded in 1989 the enlightened faction remained loyal to the National Party. Nor was this problematic, since both John Vorster and P W Botha had an ear for enlightenment at certain stages of their regimes.

John Vorster accommodated enlightenment with his move to have facilities shared by all population groups; by easing petty segregation in apartheid; by normalizing sports policy to provide for mixed sport (F W had a great deal to do with this); by undertaking to scrutinize discriminatory legislation; by giving more recognition to self-determination for blacks outside the homelands; by appointing the Theron Commission to investigate the situation of the coloured people; by making the first moves towards three parliaments for whites, coloured people and Indians, with joint decision-making on matters of mutual interest; and by many other steps that may be typified as a more relaxed and open policy.

P W Botha opted more openly for enlightenment, and his constitutional reforms were seen by the enlightened faction as a breakthrough. He also did much to promote negotiation and settlement between the government and blacks. From his Upington address, in which he spelled out his reform policy under the slogan 'adapt or die', to his last achievement in meeting Mandela, he was a man of action who worked fearlessly for a political rearrangement in South Africa. He took the decisive step towards change, and history will eventually give him full credit for that.

Via Vorster and Botha, then, enlightenment was accommodated step by step. There were some serious setbacks, too, for both leaders remained caught in the philosophy of apartheid as a basis also for reform politics.

Another reason why the enlightened movement did not launch an organized and structured action relates to the nature of the liberal mentality. Individualism, resistance to organization, a distaste for plotting, and the rejection of narrow group thinking made every enlightened person do his own thing.

All the individuals and organizations were tributaries to the mainstream that gave impetus to the political philosophy of enlightened Afrikaners. I do not want to mention names, but Church leaders, Afrikaans editors, political commentators, businessmen, Broederbond leaders, academics, and about twenty National Party parliamentarians carried the standard of Afrikaner enlightenment. Books and columns were written, closed and open meetings were addressed in all quarters, memos, proposals and reports were drafted, and delegations were led to see the authorities. Over a period of three years the ANC was met in secret. Think-tanks were attended and a network of communication channels was forced open.

Thus the enlightened movement among Afrikaners became a dynamic force that paved the way for F W de Klerk.

8

This chapter has sought to substantiate the opening statement that although February 2, 1990, did indeed represent a political leap, the National Party had been well prepared for it, and the climate, also among the Afrikaans public, was right for the F W policy.

Listening to Afrikaners and other whites of all inclinations and stations has given me the impression that the political mood after F W's policy speech could be divided into four sectors. Briefly, they are the responses of the panicky, the grovellers, the impatient, and the persevering. This classification has nothing to do with political parties; the four factions are widely spread over the whole spectrum. But I might narrow the field a bit by pointing out that all four groups are to be found among government supporters.

The panicky are motivated by fears: fear for their survival ('the blacks are going to steamroller the Afrikaners'); fear born of despair ('there is no solution to our situation, no plans will work, we are doomed'); escapist fears ('we can isolate ourselves in our own homeland, or in an enclave of self-determination'); suspicious fears ('fine talk is deceptive; once the blacks have us in a corner they are going to strike'); belligerent fear ('the Afrikaners are not going to knuckle under, we will strike back if the blacks demand too much of us'). Such fears produce aggression, heel-dragging, pessimism, and a sense of impotence.

The grovellers ooze humility. They are over-sensitive to our guilt, to our misdeeds in the history of apartheid, and to the injustice that has to be expiated. They hold out a begging-bowl and hope to be accepted, to be forgiven, to be granted a place in the sun. They lean over backwards to demonstrate their humility and their much-vaunted understanding of black passions. They are prepared to become handmaidens. To them, all black aspirations are sacrosanct and justified.

The impatient branch off in two directions. The paternalists among them mutter that the blacks should stop their 'nonsense'; since the government has leant over backwards to open doors, the blacks ought to co-operate, accept the 'offer', and drop their obstructionist tactics. The 'onus of proof' is now on them, to show whether or not they are going to co-operate. They must take what they are given, otherwise they may end up empty-handed. They mustn't think we are going to kowtow to them.

The other line taken by the impatient is that of over-simplification. Having exorcised our problems, we can quickly negotiate a kind of federation in which joint decision-making and self-determination are guaranteed for every group. This faction is convinced that the knot is as good as cut, provided the blacks are mature enough not to be the fly in the ointment. They think we need just a few more adjustments and concessions to see us through. They find it odd that the blacks are not jumping at the chances offered them.

The persevering display the paradoxical emotions of initiative and wait-and-see. They show initiative by actively supporting and promoting such moves as the rapid phasing out of apartheid, the building of a climate of trust and openness, the creation of various contact networks and negotiating forums to pave the way, a realistic weighing and measuring to find acceptable compromises for a constitution, for the economy, for labour, for education and for all other spheres in which new packages have to be designed.

This group shows initiative through planning, research, communication, the diagnosing of realities and the defining of alternative routes. They are solution-oriented and believe that solutions can be found through hard work. They take the bit between their teeth to create an acceptable future for all of us. They distinguish between what is really non-negotiable (all the values of democracy) and what is negotiable (all the remnants of apartheid). They are ready for tough negotiations and will not be caught napping.

They avoid panic, grovelling and impatience by adopting a political attitude of wait-and-see, an attitude founded on the sober realization that all change is a process. Processes have obstacles, small advances, setbacks, stalemates, confrontation, persuasion, breakthroughs ... as long as the wagon keeps rolling the drift will be crossed inch by inch. All one has to do is to hang in there, swallow the disappointments, accept the failures, patiently cope with the delays. But meanwhile, keep the shoulder to the wheel.

Finding compromise in South Africa is going to be a lengthy process. Everybody, black and white, will have to shift their focus, grind new lenses, and explore new routes. In that process there is going to be much slipping and stumbling by Afrikaners, politicians, black groupings, and whoever else is involved.

The persevering understand the rules of the game. They do not balk at short-circuits, throw in the towel, or demand shortcuts.

Are we as Afrikaners mature enough, tough enough and clear-minded enough to persevere? Finding out whether we have that perseverance is going to be our acid test.

I do not doubt for a moment that F W will persevere. He was prepared for it by the dynamics of the political development discussed in this book and specifically in this chapter. And he has made his choices, assimilating and integrating the influences that have impacted on him over the years.

F W is his own man in every sense of the word. He is too critical and too independent to be told what to do. Intellectually he is a loner who designs his own frameworks. Like anyone else, he is open to influences, and the enlightened political concepts others and I kept before him over the years, whether in discussions or in confrontations, did not pass him by.

4

THE PROFILE

1

Who is F W de Klerk?

In drawing a profile of him I am, of course, running a great risk of subjectivity, for in a relationship of many years one inevitably builds up negative and positive impressions of a man.

A tabulation of F W's weaknesses might be sensational: like all mankind, he is of a 'crooked and perverse generation', as the Bible puts it; in him, too, the negative forces of our fallen state are manifested; he, too, has his feet of clay, his irritating mannerisms, his lapses. Although there is nothing exciting from the dark side of life to pin to him – he has no ugly skeletons in the closet to gossip about – he, too, has his tally of failures and inefficiencies, of times, places and events he would dearly like to forget.

I have no intention of ferreting out these things. When it is relevant and in the public interest one has to tear down the veils; but if someone's flaws have no bearing on his efficiency in performing his duties, then he has a right to privacy, and it is our duty to respect that privacy.

In this book the criticism levelled against F W over the years is discussed: his conservative image; his over-cautious formulation of policy, attempting to cater to all sides; his non-aggressive – sometimes unnecessarily tolerant – approach; his lack of rigidity, and the conformity with all phases of National Party policy that had stamped him as a man of compromise rather than

128

30

31

30 Mr De Klerk, then still Acting State President, met President Kenneth Kaunda of Zambia in Livingstone, Zambia.
31 On his first European tour as State President he met French President François Mitterrand in Paris.

32

33

34

32 With the Portuguese Prime Minister Anibal Cavaço Silva.
33 In Greece, with Greek Prime Minister Constantine Mitsotakis (left of President De Klerk).
34 President and Mrs De Klerk with Margaret Thatcher and her husband Denis, at the then British Prime Minister's country residence Chequers.

35 With King Juan Carlos and Queen Sofia of Spain, in Madrid.
36 With Italian Prime Minister Giulio Andreotti.

35

36

37 With Helmut Kohl, the German Chancellor.

38 With Moroccan Prime Minister Azzedine Laraki at Rabat Airport before departing for the Netherlands.

37

38

39

40

39 The presidential couple with Queen Beatrix and Prince Claus of the Netherlands.
40 Washington. South Africa meets America across the conference table.

41 President De Klerk and Mr Pik Botha with President George Bush in the grounds of the White House.
42 Two presidents – De Klerk and Bush.

43 With American Vice-President Dan Quayle.
44 President and Mrs De Klerk with American Secretary of State James Baker.

a political innovator or entrepreneur. Still, to every point of criticism this book offers a response. His capacity for growth will also be discussed further. In his new office he has made the critics eat their words.

Every personality has its engaging side and its blemishes; everyone's talents have poles of competency and incompetence; every individual is caught in a dichotomy of constructive and destructive forces, of truth and falsehood, morality and immorality, strength and weakness. F W de Klerk is no exception.

I shall draw a profile of only those facets of his personality and style that will help us to gain some insight into the man who, as State President, has a leading role to play in South African politics of the nineties.

2

F W de Klerk and his times are inextricably entwined in this book.

So far we have met him in various guises: as a man who dislikes pomp and circumstance, and who does not act impulsively. He was well aware of what he was about to do to our country's politics on February 2, 1990. He was confident that it was the right thing to do, and that the exigencies of our situation demanded that leap of faith. Positive as well as negative expectations had built up around him. He could not escape his 'conservative' image and the perception that he was over-cautious, and inclined to be all things to all men. That he has shown contrary qualities since taking office has come as a surprise to one and all.

His transformation into a highly marketable media personality was remarkable. It has given him a new public identity, as it were, as a confident, calm and open person. His remarkably successful association with world leaders and the impact of his arguments on them have contributed further to his stature. At the same time he has proved himself a successful bridge-builder to his black political opponents, none of whom questions his integrity in any way.

In the pages of this book, he has emerged as pragmatic and

realistic. He has shown a remarkable ability to reconcile the different factions in the National Party, to inject new enthusiasm into a tired party, and to unite his colleagues loyally behind him.

He has shown himself to be essentially an Afrikaner with strong feelings about the future of his people and the maintenance of their rights, in spite of the vendetta against him by Afrikaners who assert the contrary.

It has become clear that, as a good politician, he read the political climate correctly and showed good timing in making his various moves. But he has also shown the stamina of a statesman in his ability to make a decision and strike out on a new course.

His style, we have seen, is conciliatory, but that he can also be confrontational is evident from the fact that he has become the foremost adversary of the Conservative Party. He has gone through different phases. Although never part of the enlightened or ultra-conservative movement among the Afrikaners, he was open and intelligent enough not to ignore the messages of the *verligtes*.

Further analysis and synthesis may show up yet more profiles.

3

F W de Klerk is capable of growth. He and others may say what they will, but the fact remains that he has undergone a political conversion. It can be defined in various ways: it is a conversion from over-cautiousness in politics to fearless entrepreneurship; from ultra-conservative leanings to outspoken enlightenment; from ideological correctness to an open, critical pragmatism and realism. That he had the capacity for political conversion is noteworthy. Our political road ahead is unknown, and in such a situation it is dangerous to be led by a stagnant person, or by one who has already reached the ceiling of his abilities.

Any South African leader – white or black – will need large reserves of vigour to cope with the future. And that is precisely what F W has proved: he can grow.

That growth does not imply mere opportunism, or trimming one's sails to the wind, nor does it mean running with the emotional currents of the moment; nor is it the random growth of a wild shoot. F W's vigour lies in healthy maturation and judicious choices. That is why his political conversion cannot be pinned down to a particular incident or the intensive pressures of a few weeks. In the language of theology – since I am using the theological term 'conversion' – it was a gradual conversion, not an instant one. Through his conversion and his vigour he has saved the National Party and South Africa from folly.

Let us consider some of the follies from which he has saved us.

The historian Barbara Tuchman discussed the follies of governments in her book *The March of Folly, from Troy to Vietnam* (1984). I would summarize her conclusion by saying that governments have done immeasurable harm through the folly of intractability. The word 'folly' encompasses foolishness, idiocy, imbecility, stupidity, and madness.

Tuchman's book identifies some of the follies of governments that the finger of history has pointed out.

Stubbornness is one: when a political situation is judged by the bias of established notions, governments become blind to contrary truths, and they and their supporters are led by wishful thinking instead of facts. Facts are pushed aside in an attempt 'to reinstate a fallen and shattered structure, turning back history'. Dead ashes are stirred up in the hope of reviving the fire of salvation.

Another folly revealed by history is the force of religious mania – a supposed divine mission, which sanctions government policy as the only resort. Tuchman speaks of 'self-hypnosis, being caught up by your own propaganda ... the self-imprisonment in the we-have-no-alternative argument'.

The book teems with examples of how an excessive reaction to opposition, an illusion of omnipotence, omnipresence, permanence and invulnerability have deluded governments and regimes into underestimating their opposition. When the wheel turns, such governments are totally unprepared to provide leadership. The result is total collapse in terms of the domino effect (as each counter tumbles, it pushes over the next one, until all have fallen).

These follies produce a style of government that Tuchman calls 'working the levers rather than thinking': leadership loses its intelligence, emotion predominates, realistic goals disappear, planning becomes haphazard, the weighing up of pros and cons becomes distorted, effectiveness is lost.

One of her conclusions: 'Rejection of reason is the prime characteristic of folly... When desire disagrees with the judgement of reason, there is a disease of the soul. And when the soul is opposed to knowledge or opinion or reason, which are her natural laws, that I call folly ... if the mind is open enough to perceive that a given policy is harming rather than serving self-interest, and self-confident enough to acknowledge it, and wise enough to reverse it, that is a summit in the art of government.'

She has traced many other follies: the abuse of power, panicky measures to allay the problem, dismissing protest as a mere aberration that can be suppressed, denying the rejection of the government's legitimacy, rigidity that compounds error instead of learning from it, incorrect information from people who are trying to curry favour. She also deals with the folly of balking on the threshold of a breakthrough, inhibited by fear and tradition.

The essence of her theme is that 'folly consisted in persistence in the pursuit, despite accumulating evidence that the goal was unattainable – folly is refusal to draw conclusions from the evidence, addiction to the counter-productive'.

It is some consolation that we are not the only ones to have made such mistakes. From Troy to Vietnam, the follies of governments and subjects are legion. The warning is that we should learn from history. Stubbornness, missions, illusions, raw emotion, power, inflexibility, fear and ignoring realities would push this country over the edge.

F W's growth and political conversion – one of the themes of this book – came none too soon. Our country was well and truly entangled in some of the follies Tuchman identifies.

The conservative ideals of partition, the government's dream of a federation in which races would form the building-blocks of the constitution and of society, the liberal opposition, who would have us believe that all ethnic concerns have to vanish before the simple majority principle, and the ANC family that wants to build a country on Marxism and socialism – these are absolutes that will not put things in order.

Reason is the key to formulating attainable ideals and realistic strategies. They can be achieved only through wide-ranging compromises between black and white, between systems of government, and between divergent political sentiments.

It may sound strange, but we shall have to think less 'purely' if we are to find solutions in the grey world of pragmatic compromise, where everyone gets something but no-one gets everything.

It is precisely towards these solutions that F W became converted.

4

F W de Klerk is undoubtedly a typical politician with the general profile of politicians all over the world, but he also has peculiarities that distinguish him from the typical politician. He fits in somewhere in the following profile of the career politician:

Every profession – politician, journalist, clergyman, academic – has a psychological character that attracts certain people; and the profession, in turn, shapes the person's profile.

At first glance, politicians strike one as carefree people, ever hopeful. They find everything important at a particular moment, but the next moment it is replaced by something else. They are sociable, kind-hearted, amiable, jovial and sympathetic, imposing, energetic people with an overwhelming presence. They focus on the practical and the concrete. They are doers who measure things by their usefulness, idealists who give their all for a cause.

If one looks at politicians through the psychological lens, the picture becomes clearer. Politicians are absolutists. They see only white or black, with no shades of grey. They are either for or against. They are authoritarian personalities who like to be in command and demand obedience. That is why politicians are suspicious: living in fear of rejection, they are hypersensitive to criticism and constantly involved in petty in-fighting aimed at short-term victories.

Analysts of political communication – much research has been done on this – point out that politicians are generally under pressure from five situations that direct their actions:

Conflict is the constant companion of the politician. The different factions in his party, public pressure groups, international consequences, and the sword of his electorate's voting patterns – all of these breed conflict, which he handles by reassuringly putting out the fires.

Since he is haunted by rivalry, by adversaries lurking around every corner, it becomes second nature to be on the offensive.

Consensus is his heart's desire. Political supporters have to be kept together. The politician is an entrepreneur of compromise, skilled in placating divergent groups.

Urgency, always an element of politics, makes crisis his bedfellow.

Timing becomes his watchword. All his communication is calculated, even if his tongue often runs away with him. The 'climate of the times' is the compass. For him, everything runs in cycles, episodes and moments. His world is a theatre in which the curtain goes up and the actor must take his bow.

There are also people who do research on the nature of political words. Typical of the language of politics, they say, is that you have to listen carefully to what politicians' words conceal. They use code words with broad connotations. In the USA, for example, the single word 'busing' connotes forced integration, violence in schools, long distances to school, discomfort, group conflict, et cetera. Listen carefully to our political code words too, because they mean more than they say: power-sharing, group rights, minorities, identity, spatial orientation.

Political language also uses euphemisms ('corrective education' means retaliatory punishment, 'relaxed talks' means not much was achieved, and 'no comment' can mean anything:

134

anger, embarrassment, concealment, rejection, agreement). Since it is usually vague and ambiguous, one should always read between the lines.

Another framework of the politician is the 'halo effect' and 'hero effect'. When an important politician speaks, it lends an aura of importance to what he says, because he makes it sound so weighty and it is backed up by others, especially by a servile press. Thus even the mediocre acquires a halo of importance.

The 'hero effect' is achieved by constantly opposing friend and foe, villains and heroes, doom and salvation, scapegoat and saviour. The politician and his cause expose the conspiracy and smite the enemy.

Politicians will always be with us. They affect every individual, every group, every part of our future and the world's. That is why we should try to understand how their minds work.

As I have said, F W fits somewhere into this profile. Mercifully, he differs from the average politician: as I have said earlier in this book, he is not a Dada. I do not know where I got the word from. It rings a bell as one of Idi Amin's official titles. To me, 'Dada' is akin to names such as Big Brother, Boss, Führer, Ayatollah or Papa. Dada is a name for anyone who relishes his power. And Dada's power has some deadly stings in its tail. Dada campaigns for a cause which he presents as sacred and exalted. He believes he is clairvoyant and knows best what is good, right, nice, virtuous and correct. He enforces his will through authority and control, because he has a messianic certainty.

In his own eyes Dada is incapable of error, and anyone who points out a mistake to him will bear the brunt of his outrage and his revenge. And he is dangerous, because he rewards and punishes on impulse.

In my files I have a article on *'Narcissistic rage in leaders'* (from *The International Journal of Social Psychiatry*, 1988, Vol. 34, No. 2, pp. 135–141, by F Mardi *et al*). I quote a few paragraphs to indicate what Dada does when he gets angry:

Suetonius, in *The Lives of the Twelve Caesars*, described emperors such as Caligula and Nero whose names are synonymous with corruption, caprice and ultimate self-destruction. In the twentieth century, Hitler and Mussolini shared many of the same attributes, which included the use of states of rage to intimidate subordinates. Such tyrants had a partial correspondence between their inner fantasies of omnipotence and their actual external power. Nevertheless, we infer that their inner psychodynamics also involved a fundamentally damaged self-concept, and that this might be why any action which appeared to cast doubt on the leader's omnipotence was savagely punished.

Because of this situation, all independent thinkers must eventually leave the inner circle of advisers of such leaders. They will tend to be replaced by individuals whose primary objective is keeping the leader pleased. In order to keep the leader serene, bad news, however true, is either not presented or is presented in such a way that a scapegoat other than the leader can be found and punished.

What is so dramatically seen in the famous continues to be found at a more ordinary level of leadership. Although injuring far fewer people than is the case with a head of state, narcissistic executives still impair institutions or individual lives through the destructiveness of bullying rages.

Self-righteous rages are states of mind related to a continuum including fear of humiliation and chronic embitterment.

Self-righteous rage occurs when a person who is usually composed becomes intensely, vengefully hostile as an exaggerated response to an insult. Violence – physical or verbal – often exceeds the usual standards of acceptable behavior, but for the moment the perpetrator feels justified.

This kind of rage is described as narcissistic because it is triggered by insults to self-esteem and because during the height of the rage others are assigned an inferior, nonhuman status. It is sometimes called 'blind hatred' because of a destructive readiness to injure others on the grounds that they have no right to survive if the self is diminished.

Other states often found in conjunction with self-righteous rage include a mixed state of shame-rage-anxiety, a state of chronic embitterment, and a state of withdrawn, numb apathetic dullness.

The self-righteous rage state is characterized by a full-bodied and sometimes exhilarating expression of towering indignation.

See, Dada is ubiquitous because he acknowledges no limits to his authority. He pries into everything: he cares little for things such as individual freedom, criticism, open discussion, other points of view, and options, all of which he dismisses, with three capital letters, as a Deviation from the Commandment under his Authority. Dada pretends to be god – in the lower case, of course, because at times Dada pretends to be pious and humble. But never, never will he give way and be weak. In Dada's dictionary, humaneness and forgiveness are libel.

Dada is inclined to be Daddy first, then Dad, then Dada, and before you know it he has become like Van Wyk Louw's Raka: 'And never again would anyone dare to shut the narrow gate against him.'

I have spent a few paragraphs on Dada for three reasons: we have had some experience of Dada in South Africa, and it was disastrous; we have to be on our guard and not tolerate any Dada, from whichever political group he may emerge; and by way of contrast I wanted to draw F W de Klerk's profile as precisely and definitely an anti-Dada person and leader.

He has traits that match the general profile of a politician, but on Dada he is an exception. His authority rests easily on him, because he is not the type to get a swollen head. He is not power-oriented. His modesty is sincere. He is familiar with doubt and fairness. He is not arrogant. Bitterness, anger and hatred are not his forte. He is not given to tantrums. He can take criticism.

He is criticized for not being aggressive enough. Let it be so; that is his nature. Sham aggression is odious. After all these years I know that he does have creative aggression, in the sense that he sticks to his will and his views with courtesy and good humour and brings others around through negotiation and persuasion. That – and only that – is healthy aggression.

F W is a conciliator who is mature enough to know that the solution often lies in healthy compromise.

His credibility is rooted in his honesty. Because he is not a Dada, he is very calm, and this calm is his outstanding characteristic.

For all these reasons, he is the right man for the South African politics of the nineties.

5

Seen from a different angle, F W has developed his own gravitas. (Gravitas is the root of words such as 'gravity'.) Not that he has always had it. Gravitas is not an inborn quality, for depth can be achieved only through hard practice and discipline.

Gravitas has to do with maturity. It grows with ripeness and from exposure to reality seen through a wide-angled lens. Gravitas flows from culture and refinement.

Sincerity, power and authority have become characteristic of F W, unrelated to any particular office or status.

Gravitas people have a magnetic field. One senses them as a presence and an abstraction. They are penetrating and reserved. There is a force behind what they do not say, and lucidity in what they do say. They have a natural dignity, but they are not ponderous; instead, they are even playful. Their intelligence, intuition, experience and wisdom, patience and humaneness give them gravitas.

F W has his own typical charisma. It does not lie in exceptionally strong individualism, in a kind of 'deviation' from normal behaviour, in uniqueness, in a quality which is almost 'unrepeatable'. Some charismatic people and leaders have the potential to become 'characters' and mythological figures. They are usually controversial; they have the ability to shock, to move and to alienate. Their statements become winged words, because their unique style derives from the exceptional force of their language, phrases and expression. Prime examples of a charismatic politician were Winston Churchill and our own John Vorster.

F W's charisma lies in his rationality, logic and balance. He has sincerity, persuasiveness, serenity and juristic preciseness, and these have undoubtedly contributed to his gravitas. He is known as an outstanding debater who has developed logical argument into a powerful weapon. And he uses this power with charm.

Research done by Hennie Kotzé and Deon Geldenhuys, professors of political science at the University of Stellenbosch and the Rand Afrikaans University respectively, and published in *Leadership* (Volume Nine, July, 1990, pp. 12–28), confirms what I have said about F W de Klerk, the person, in this chapter.

They distinguish the following as typical of the De Klerk style: He has a consultative style, which includes an open-door approach and listening to colleagues and subordinates; a democratic style that seeks consensus through consultation; a style of team-work and team-building that has given new status to the corporate responsibility of the cabinet as a decision-making authority; a rational style of decision-making that collects information, analyses it intellectually, summarizes the essence of the matter, and weighs up different options; a negotiating style that relies on compromise and persuasion; a style carried by informality, sincerity, integrity, friendliness and modesty.

They wrote: 'The difference in political style between F W de Klerk and P W Botha was neatly summed up by a seasoned newspaperman: "Where President Botha is rough, he is smooth; where President Botha smashes, he leads; where President Botha confronts and rages, he yields and mollifies. His career is a tale of compromises, making the best of bad situations, of smoothing over difficulties." '

6

As the tree is the product of its root-system, so is the adult largely the product of his upbringing.

F W de Klerk's political roots run far and deep. His paternal great-grandfather was Senator Jan van Rooy, who played an active role in the politics of his day and had a strong influence on F W's father, Senator Jan de Klerk, because little Jan was the apple of his grandfather's eye. He died when Jan was well into his thirties. F W's grandfather, Willem de Klerk, was one of those rare politically active clergymen, who left a further impression on our father, Jan. Willem, our grandfather, was a Cape Rebel during the Anglo-Boer War; he twice stood for the National Party in Potchefstroom but lost both times to the old South African Party. In later years he was honorary chairman of the National Party on the Witwatersrand, a regular speaker at political meetings, and a volunteer part-time administrative assistant at the National Party newspaper *Die Transvaler*. Grandpa Willem, a prominent political figure in the Transvaal, played a leading role behind the scenes to build up the National Party. And then there was our father, Jan, who was an active politician for 31 years – as secretary of the National Party in the Transvaal, member of the Transvaal Provincial Council and of the Executive Committee, a member of the cabinet for 15 years in the governments of Strydom, Verwoerd and Vorster, and President of the Senate for seven years. He was a highly respected and influential man.

F W's aunt, his father's sister Susan, was married to Hans Strijdom, leader of the National Party in the Transvaal and later Prime Minister, a man who became symbol and myth as a campaigner for the political voice of the Afrikaner and the ideal of an independent republic.

On his mother's side, his grandfather, F W Coetzer, was a member of the Free State Provincial Council for many years. I, his brother, have been involved in political commentary since 1966, and was editor and columnist for the papers *Die Transvaler* and *Rapport* for 15 years.

F W, one could say, was genetically predestined to become a politician. He did not fall into it by chance; politics is part of his heritage. But this background also formed part of his political 'education'. His exposure to the inner circles of politics, both as a child and as a young man, gave him an early political sophistication.

We often talked politics at home; political public figures were regular guests; even as children and students we, and particularly he, were involved in the organization of election campaigns; as a young man he attended dozens of political meetings with our father; and he was involved in many a late night political argument, when I confronted father and brother with enlightened politics, which led to some spirited debates.

In a manner of speaking, he was predestined for politics by his collective subconscious, via his lineage, and honed for the task by his political parentage. And that was also where he acquired his deep loyalty to the National Party.

Of course, upbringing – his too – is more than just politics; it is everything one's parents give one, at all levels. F W had a secure childhood, because his parents, Jan and Corrie, were 'nice' parents: loving and interested in their children, involving them in everything as though they were friends. It was a comfortable, spontaneous home, with lots of laughter and cosiness, entertainment and holidays, quarrels and reconciliation – a typical 'one-for-all-and-all-for-one' atmosphere of closeness and tolerance.

In analysing his upbringing I found it revealing to note how the lines of his education can be traced through his personal and political life.

Love was given generously, openly and demonstratively. F W is a loving man who hugs and cuddles. A sense of proportion was inculcated into us. Excesses had to be avoided; the pattern was anti-extremism, anti-fanaticism, anti-overstatement. 'Doe gewoon, dat's gek genoeg' (act normally – that's quite mad enough) was our father's Dutch maxim. And F W is exactly that: an ordinary, balanced person who avoids one-sidedness.

His parents did not push their children. Authority, rules, regulations, discipline, achievement, standing to attention, were played down in his upbringing. F W is easy and relaxed, almost phlegmatic, and free from anxiety and excitability. His parents built up his confidence by emphasizing that one should accept oneself, develop one's own individuality, and become one's own person. Yet one should remain modest, because another of his father's Dutch sayings was that one should never tell oneself: 'Aap, wat ben je een mooie jonge'. (Monkey, what a splendid chap you are.) F W has no delusions of grandeur. His modesty is genuine, yet he is aware of the self one should remain true to.

His father was a master conversationalist who could get on with anyone in any company. The salt and pepper of his humour made him the soul of many an informal gathering. His mother is more reserved, shy and reticent. F W has both traits – exuberant joviality and reticence. He is more of an introvert than an extrovert.

Hard work was the order of the day in his parental home, and it was done with commitment and purpose, each task taken on and carried out methodically and neatly. And F W is known for his hard work, stamina and methodical approach.

The tree is indeed the product of its roots.

A question often asked is how our father Jan, who for many years was a key figure in South African politics, formed the political philosophy of his sons. Was he not the archetypal ultra-conservative? The answer is no, not within the context of his time. Granted, he was one of the originators and implementers of rigid apartheid, but in that he was in line with nearly 90 per cent of Afrikaners from the forties to the beginning of the eighties. In the context of his time he was open to reform and change. He was not dogmatic or fanatical.

F W learned his blind loyalty to the National Party from his father. Our family shared the Afrikaner sentiment against injustice, oppression and the suppression of political and economic ideals. We were raised to believe passionately that the British hegemony in South Africa should be rejected and that the National Party was the front that would redress the 'century of injustice'. When the party came to power in 1948 euphoria ran high. In F W's political education National Party principles were never questioned: political leaders were followed heart and soul and there was never any doubt that every single aspect of policy was correct, logical and the only option.

This undoubtedly formed F W as a National Party loyalist and it has been a trademark of his entire political career. The changes in his political philosophy after 1986 continued to be in line with changes within the party.

In the same home, his brother Willem developed a resistance to the uncritical acceptance of apartheid. Partly out of reaction and partly out of an underlying philosophical attitude and relativistic view of the world, our paths began gradually to diverge. Father Jan and F W were bound in conformity with apartheid and I in disillusionment with apartheid, though still within the framework of the *verligte* wing of the National Party, until the last two years of P W Botha's rule led to my break with the party. These political differences brought tension to our home. But under the watchful eye of mother Corrie, with her tolerance of independence and individuality, and her sense of balance, there was still room for our divergent views.

Since then, following the leaps of the National Party and F W in the dismantling of apartheid, the brothers are once again, politically, of the same mind.

Later in his life, especially in the last few years, our father realized that drastic changes to apartheid must be made and started to speak out in favour of reforming certain aspects. The fact that his father became critical of the system definitely sowed a seed in F W.

What did the 'apartheid family' of the De Klerks look like? Among foreigners, in particular, the impression exists that Afrikaner homes are fired by rancour, hate, suppression and exploitation of black people. This was in no respect the case. As in every South African home, there was a master-servant relationship that was typically colonial and paternalistic. We grew up with the rules of fairness, honesty and charity to the black people in our household. A relaxed and friendly association, taking care of their needs, made an involvement that drew everyone together into a 'greater family'.

There is some common bond between Afrikaners and black people that is part of the fabric of this country's tradition – but always within the boundaries of apartheid: you did not live together, eat together, sleep together; you did not socialize or worship in the same churches, and you were not partners in political decisions.

Like many Afrikaners, F W de Klerk has slowly outgrown apartheid.

7

In the context of family and friendship one gets to know a man in his nakedness, his ups and downs, his irritations and selfishness, his demonstrations, emotions, preferences and eccentricities. The man without the mask – that is how one is seen by family and friends.

A summary of interviews with his wife, Marike, and with his three children (Jan, the eldest, is a farmer in the Western Transvaal; Willem, the middle child, is in public relations; and Susan, his daughter, is a teacher) shows total agreement on one point:

143

F W is intensely involved, interested, encouraging, and always overly concerned for their well-being. He makes time to give them quality in listening to their problems, in conversations with them, and in their many gatherings as a family, even if only for a few hours. He phones every week to ask how they are. And he is the happiest of grandfathers. Yes, he is strict, but never unreasonable; he gets angry but never loses control; he gives straightforward advice but is never prescriptive. He is considerate, a true gentleman, and keeps the atmosphere in their home light. He inspires them by building their confidence and being appreciative rather than critical. Even in a bad mood he is never unfair.

When F W himself talks about his family, one is struck by the warmth in his eyes and voice: 'My wife and children are like a fortress around me. Without their love and consideration I would have been in a muddle. Since early times I have been very busy and often away from home. But I was determined not to become the absent husband and father. So I spend a lot of quality time with my family. We plan evenings and weekends together, we communicate regularly by telephone, we share each other's burdens and joys. The closeness of our relationships is very important to me.

'I have always had Marike's whole-hearted support. She is my left and my right hand, and we fit together like hand and glove. I have the highest regard for her inputs in all aspects of our household and in my work as politician and State President.'

Marike's maiden name was Willemse. Her father was a professor at the University of Pretoria and she obtained a B.Comm. degree at Potchefstroom University. They were young when they got married in 1959 – F W was 23 and she 22.

I would summarize her profile as follows: an attractive woman with excellent taste in fashion, interior decorating, her table settings, flower arranging and many other things that make her person and her home something special; a conscientious woman who punctiliously completes whatever she takes on; she has a particularly sharp intellect which she applies over a broad spectrum, from politics to art, literature and economics; a woman

144

who tolerates no nonsense, very straightforward and out-spoken, with no hypocrisy or beating about the bush, direct; independent and incisive in her thinking, with an academic approach; yet she is a committed person with strong feelings about people and issues, religion, norms and values, sorrow and suffering; she is service-oriented and very successfully combines her duties as wife and mother with the agenda of a professional woman.

Marike's relationship with F W is also that of a partnership. She has contributed enormously to building up the National Party's women's movement. She travels widely and has made a name for herself as a public speaker who is as much at home behind the microphone as F W himself.

F W and Marike have a wide circle of friends. And these are not fair-weather friends: old friends from their university days and new friends have united in a community who are loyal to them and are at home with them as only people who have known each other for a long time can be.

8

F W de Klerk is a man of strong principles. In his outlook on life, it seems to me, he is a firmly rooted man, and those roots can be defined in two words: he is an Afrikaner Calvinist.

The connotations of this term – Afrikaner Calvinist – have not been and are still not very positive. It has been distorted into a caricature of people who are primitive and inflexible by nature, heavily conservative and rigid in thought and action, closed people, who have entrenched themselves in isolation as a 'chosen' people, more or less like Israel in the Old Testament, with whom they identify.

There are also somewhat friendlier connotations to the term Afrikaner Calvinist, but always with a sting in the tail. This friendlier form of criticism maintains that Afrikaner Calvinists are religious fundamentalists, sticklers for principles, stiff and traditionalistic, inspired by a narrow nationalism. They are so nation-bound that the Afrikaner nation has become their highest value, which is why they are inclined towards exclusivism and definitely also towards racial prejudice. The prototype of Afrikaner Calvinism, seen like this, is the Conservative Party mentality.

I would not reject that portrayal out of hand. Calvinism has traces of the typical 'paternalistic religions', which place strong emphasis on law, order, discipline, uniformity, calling and exclusivity. Its tendency to draw boundaries has certainly contributed to the apartheid policy, with its divisions between races, each with its own freedom and voice.

In addition to Calvinism, the history of the Afrikaner has also created a type of national character. Afrikaners have experience of being under threat and of being wronged by the traumas of their history of domination. Their isolation, over many decades, from the influence of world culture, the vastness of the country, their small numbers and their rural existence, with its typical culture, have given the Afrikaners a dimension of closedness. History has strengthened their herd-mentality with strong tendencies towards suspicion and cautiousness. Although there is also a tradition of divisiveness, the almost mystical pursuit of unity remains. The years of political domination in South Africa have also given the Afrikaners a kind of arrogance in staking their claims, a possessiveness, and a paternalistic piety; so that they have tended to project themselves as the true nucleus of this country's population.

To typify F W de Klerk's outlook on life as that of an Afrikaner Calvinist could, therefore, evoke negative images – and those images are not necessarily false.

Nevertheless, I would typify him as an Afrikaner Calvinist, with the footnote that there are different types of Afrikaner Calvinist. Some of the distinctions that have done the rounds are: ultra-conservative as opposed to enlightened Afrikaner Calvinists; stereotyped Afrikaners who entrench themselves in a monistic culture and group identification, as against the compromising Afrikaner whose adaptability makes him broaden his identity; the liberal Afrikaner who has broken free of the 'truths of his people'; the mature Afrikaner who does not hold with an 'obsolete identity' and rejects ready-made and stock answers; the cultural Afrikaner whose point of departure is not group nationalism but cultural identity, free of ethnicity, and who wants to build a new nation under an overarching South Africanism unfettered by colour and race.

I would make the general statement – leaving aside the different types – that a significant number of Afrikaners, including Calvinists, have broken through isolation and exclusiveness, have turned their backs on apartheid, and are exposing themselves fully to the more modern lifestyles and patterns of thought. Yet they remain Calvinists.

F W is one of these modern Afrikaners. And yet, despite all the foregoing, I maintain that he is an Afrikaner Calvinist.

The basis of Calvinism is the view that all of reality, at all levels of life, has to be subject to the authority of Biblical principles. And that is precisely what F W's philosophy of life comprises. He believes in God and in the authority of the Bible as the revealed will of God. That is why he tries to remain true to the Bible in all dimensions of his existence, and that is why his political credo is founded on justice.

Calvinism places strong emphasis on the church as institutionalized communication between God and man. F W is a regular church-goer and makes his private home life an altar of Biblical study and prayer. His Calvinism, inherited from his furthest paternal and maternal forbears, made him a member of the Gereformeerde Kerk ('Reformed' Church). Colloquially known as the 'Dopper' Church, it is the smallest of the three Afrikaans churches. The culture of the 'Dopper' Church is distinguished by strong emphasis on the dogmatic and realistic aspects of religion and by a sober-mindedness that rejects fanaticism.

Churchism – claiming that your church is the true church, and giving preference to members of your church in appointments to positions in society – has been and still is very common in South Africa. Our history has seen bitter feuds fought and harsh statements made (sometimes ostensibly in jest) about who belongs to which church. That association has often determined appointments, be it in education, in the public service, or to a public position. The 'Doppers', as the smallest group, can justly claim to have suffered their share of discrimination. Yet this church has produced a multitude of influential individuals in the history of the Afrikaner.

Churchism is definitely on the wane in our society. The Afrikaner has been confronted by other problems, and churchism has become a luxury. Religious denomination played no role in F W's election as leader of the National Party and as State President. There were some reservations about his being a 'Dopper', but the highest factor was the conviction that religious denomination was irrelevant. A contributing factor was that F W had never practised any form of churchism. In this regard he has a clean record.

F W is an Afrikaner Calvinist also in his view that a state cannot be neutral. Freedom of religion is a Calvinist principle he would never violate, but the Calvinistic imperative that the state respect and promote Christianity is also part of his philosophy of life.

Calvinism has an age-old principle defined as sovereignty within one's own sphere, a concept embracing the highly valued Calvinist idea of freedom. The individual, the church, the family, the state, institutions, the nation – each has its own rights and duties. No institution may dominate another. Each institution has its own foundation and destiny, which have to be recognized and preserved. This philosophy of life also gives F W a specific perspective on the Afrikaner nation, as a group of people who have a right to their identity, are bound by their common heritage, history, language and culture, and are entitled to a say in the future in South Africa because it is their fatherland too.

For him it is a question of principle. There must be no tampering with our right to our identity. Afrikaners are a proud people, tried and tested by the hardships of the past and compelled by that past to assert themselves. Afrikaners, too, are an African tribe, rooted in the harshness and mystery of this continent. Afrikanerdom – like the other ethnic groups in the country

– is a reality, with a claim not only to cultural identity but also to political participation.

A common South African loyalty in one state does not exclude the ethnic heritage and composition of the country.

Calvinism acknowledges paradoxes and seemingly conflicting facets of the same truth. That is why F W is confidently, unashamedly an Afrikaner, yet at the same time a South African. He has reconciled the centripetal and centrifugal forces in our politics.

Yet another feature of F W's philosophy is the Calvinistic concept of a mission, the conviction that the individual and the group have a specific function in history. Gravity and commitment, working and serving, fulfilling your task, having a calling, being predestined for your task in life and being accountable are concepts that shape the pattern of his life.

In his philosophy of life, then, he is an Afrikaner Calvinist.

9

No dramatic or traumatic events have disrupted F W de Klerk's career. The course of his life is marked by success and achievement.

He was born in Mayfair, Johannesburg, on March 18, 1936, the second son of Jan – then a teacher – and Corrie de Klerk. The family is made up of two boys, with an eight-year age gap between them.

Since he changed schools seven times in seven years, it is surprising that he maintained his level of achievement in primary school. This extraordinary shuttling from school to school was the result of our father's political activities, which necessitated constant moving. His primary school report cards did not suffer, however; they showed an average of 80 per cent and above every year.

He was a boarder at Monument High School, Krugersdorp, until he obtained a first-class matric pass in 1953. It was a great disappointment that he did not get the four distinctions all his teachers had expected. He himself blames this, his worst examination ever, on tennis, being in love with a blonde girl, and boredom with his school work. Even in high school he excelled as the prime debater of the debating society, and he remembers that Latin was his favourite subject because of its analytical nature.

From 1954 to 1958 he studied at Potchefstroom University, where he obtained Bachelor of Arts and Bachelor of Law degrees. He excelled academically but also played an energetic and leading role in student movements, serving as editor of the student newspaper, as vice-chairman of the student council, and as chairman and national executive committee member of the political-cultural Afrikaanse Studentebond, as well as on the National Party's Youth Council, of which he was the chairman, and in a string of other organizations.

It was clear even then that F W was a political person, a man for organizations and a community-oriented leader, yet also a man for relaxation: his friends still tell stories of F W as a joker and the soul of every party, as an avid tennis player and a rather less successful hockey player, something of a ladies' man, and a jovial ringleader in student merry-making.

He still regards his legal studies as an unforgettable experience and likes to refer to himself as a legal man. As he puts it, 'I found law studies absorbing because of their exactness, the thorough analysis and the foundation of principles that underpins each legal subject. The insights and methods of thought inculcated in me by my studies have become part of my way of life. The underlying principle of justice, the high regard for the judiciary, the sovereignty of the law, and the judicial settlement of disputes have become part of my political philosophy. My style remains that of an advocate, of argument and counter-argument, of weighing up truth and falsehood, justice and injustice.'

His university girlfriend, Marike Willemse, became his wife in 1959.

After university, he entered the legal profession as an articled clerk with the firm Pelser in Klerksdorp. (Peet Pelser, incidentally, also later became a politician and a cabinet minister. F W recalls that they talked more politics than law during his apprenticeship.) Then he became an articled clerk with the firm MacRobert in Pretoria. In 1962 he set up his own partnership in Vereeniging and built it up to an enormous success within ten years. He made a name for himself as a lawyer: his partners call him 'the clear head', a man who can place a case in context in no time at all.

His service to the community was not diminished by his professional workload. He was the national chairman of the Junior Rapportryers for two years and chairman of the law society of the Vaal Triangle. He served on the council of the local technikon, on the church council, on the school board and in other cultural organizations. And, of course, as chairman and leader of political committees.

Then he became restless and decided to accept the offer of a professorship of law at his Alma Mater. This was in 1972.

What was his motivation? F W explains: 'We had just returned from a trip abroad. I was able to look at my work from a distance, and I realized I did not want to be restricted to a lawyer's office: I felt the urge to contribute on a broader basis. I jumped at the offer to become an academic, because I wanted to expand my horizons. But I knew it would only be an interim step.'

Before he could take up the professorship a vacancy for Parliament arose in Vereeniging. He was approached immediately and, after consultation with the university, accepted the offer to become the candidate for the National Party – all within two days. On November 29, 1972, he was elected to the House of Assembly. That was the beginning of his full-time career as a politician.

When I asked around among his colleagues of the time and among veterans who remember him as a back-bencher in Parliament, six De Klerk achievements were singled out:

Within weeks he became known as an excellent debater who argued at a high level and with cold logic. He soon became a formidable opponent in debate, who lost no opportunity to drive the opposition into a corner. At this level, his rise was phenomenal; still a junior, he was deployed in complex and critical debates.

He also soon became an influential member of the National Party's parliamentary study groups, including those on the consolidation of the homelands, on labour, justice and home affairs. As someone put it: 'F W was always well briefed. He did his homework thoroughly. His lucidity was remarkable.'

His third achievement was that he became information officer of the Transvaal National Party fairly early in his career, and later also a member of the party's federal information service. As marketer of the policy, or as propagandist, let us say, he impressed everyone who worked with him.

He also played a key role in two select committees, one of which formulated a new policy on the opening of hotels to non-whites and the other a new censorship law that broke away from the inflexibility of the old Act. He did much to eliminate the ultra-conservative elements from censorship legislation.

F W played a leading role in another area too: the National Party launched a new youth movement, which still forms a basic element of the party structure.

His sixth achievement was the many invitations from abroad that he received as a member of parliamentary groups – to Germany, England, America and Israel. He himself says that these visits greatly helped him to develop an overseas perspective. His colleagues recall that he virtually became the spokesman of the team in the intensive political discussions on these trips.

He was very popular in his constituency, because he listened to people's problems. A man who was ready to serve, and a hard worker, one of his political friends from Vereeniging called him.

Of his 'back-bench' years (I put it in inverted commas, because he had front-bench status and did front-bench work), F W says: 'I worked very hard. What I valued most was the many informal discussions with colleagues. We young ones discussed all aspects of political policy from morning till night.' And the young ones of the time tell me that even then they recognized F W as an authority.

Speaking of the young ones – it is still to F W's credit that he will not be drawn into cliques. He was never part of conspiracies or pressure groups; he cherished his independence.

Prime Minister John Vorster took note of F W. In 1975, he informed me that F W would one day become Prime Minister. Of course I told my parents and F W about the compliment; that is why I remember it so well. F W told me that Vorster had always treated him with great warmth, even a kind of fatherliness. Even after his resignation and the crisis of the information scandal, when he was deeply embittered, the bond between him and F W was never broken.

The secret can now be told that Vorster wanted to promote F W to deputy minister in January, 1976. The message was relayed to our father and to F W and had been leaked to the press. Our father rented a suite in a Cape Town hotel for a family celebration. Twelve hours before it was to have been announced, the message came through that it would no longer happen. Dr A P Treurnicht was promoted instead and rumour had it that he had even then been identified as a 'troublesome' man who had to be promoted to keep him quiet. There had obviously been pressure from the Treurnicht group, but it was never admitted.

F W de Klerk got his promotion – directly to Minister of Social Welfare and Pensions – on April 3, 1978. At 42 he was one of the youngest ministers ever.

His first cabinet meeting was historical in the sense that UN resolution 435 on South-West Africa was accepted by the government at that meeting.

In each of F W's portfolios he did pioneering work. As Minister of Sport he depoliticized sport and restored full autonomy to sporting control bodies; as Minister of Post and Telecommunications he finalized the contracts that led South Africa into the electronic era; as Minister of Mining he formulated our policy on coal exports and on the structuring of Eskom and the Atomic Energy Corporation; as Minister of the Interior he handled the repeal of the Mixed Marriages Act; and as Minister of National Education he extended the department into an umbrella department that included all groups, and laid the founda-

153

tions for a single educational system and for co-ordinating structures.

F W de Klerk was never part of P W Botha's inner circle. At a later stage there was in fact some tension between them, yet he is most appreciative of P W Botha as an administrative and constitutional reformer, as a strategist in national security, and as a man who made a decisive contribution to ensuring independence for Namibia.

A noteworthy part of F W's career is his exceptional efforts in rebuilding the National Party in the Transvaal after the break with Dr A P Treurnicht and his group in 1982. As new Transvaal leader he was left with the legacy of Dr Treurnicht's resignation: a shattered party, internecine squabbling, and despondency. Under F W's leadership, one constituency after another was scrutinized to separate the sheep from the goats. Regional committees and branches had to be built up from scratch, fundraising drives had to be launched, information campaigns had to allay confusion and douse the flames. It was an exhausting task that demanded patience and persuasiveness. The success achieved testifies to F W's flair for conciliation, persuasion and organization.

No wonder he received the Decoration for Meritorious Service in 1981. When he was awarded an honorary doctorate from Potchefstroom University on September 21, 1990, the university motivated the award as follows in its official programme *(translated)*: 'The highest award the University can make is the presentation of the degree Doctor of Law (*Honoris Causa*), whereby recognition is given to Mr de Klerk: for his achievements in his legal career; for his election as State President, and for the statesmanship he has shown in this high office; for his strong yet conciliatory efforts to bring about peace; for the clear reflection of his Christian principles in his thought and vision as a leader; for the way in which he accepted the responsibility of leadership to establish a constitutional dispensation in which justice and the elimination of racial discrimination shall be key elements; and for the faith in God, acknowledgement of depen-

154

dence and awareness of a mission that he has brought to the execution of his office.'

His curriculum vitae shows that the State President is a man of success who makes things happen.

10

In this chapter a profile has emerged of a hardworking man, one who is fully equipped for his task as a political leader at this stage in the history of South Africa's development.

But F W knows that man cannot live by work alone. In many ways he is also a man of leisure, with healthy relaxations that give him physical and mental stamina.

Unfortunately, and to the dismay of many people, he is a chain-smoker. Like all nicotine addicts he plays it down by rationalising that he is one of those fortunate ones who suffer no ill effects from smoking. He often quotes one of his father's Dutch sayings: 'Een tevreden roker is geen onruststoker.' (A happy smoker is never a trouble-maker.) Who knows, perhaps some doctor will 'convert' him in this respect too.

In company he relaxes easily with a glass of whisky or wine and sociable small-talk. He is not a political animal who only talks politics; in fact, he has a remarkable knack for doffing his political cap and chatting entertainingly about everything on earth. His hearty laugh, the gourmet food he so enjoys and the string of jokes he has at his fingertips make him a carefree man in his leisure time.

Regular games of golf (at which he performs indifferently), hunting trips (he is a fair shot), brisk walks for exercise, and weekends and holidays, some spent at his beach house in Hermanus, stimulate his circulation and calm his mind.

5

THE ROAD AHEAD

1

There are no prophets any more. A modern-day Nostradamus would have been hard put to predict scenarios for South Africa in his conundrums.

The various scenarios doing the rounds range from Utopia to Armageddon, interspersed with cautious optimism and cautious pessimism. The problem with scenarios is that they work with probabilities and possibilities, weighed and calculated mathematically and deterministically. The element of surprise, the sudden turn, the radical trauma, the positive revolution, can shatter the neat framework of scenarios.

This point was well illustrated when F W came to power. During the last two years of the P W Botha regime it was the vogue to call in scenario experts to read the cards. Short-term predictions piled abyss on abyss. After a year of De Klerk government the whole scene changed, and most scenarios lost their relevance. Then the hip-hip-hurray scenarios did the rounds. Still later, when new violence broke out in the townships, sanctions against South Africa were not lifted, and the ANC struggled to get a grip on the black masses, the prophets once again began looking at the country through dark glasses.

I am not scoffing at the science of scenario planning; it is essential to effective management to try to predict the future and lay down your strategies for any eventuality. I will not try my hand at scenarios in this chapter, however; I shall rather jot down some notes on the process, as I see it, that F W has to guide and share, which will hopefully lead us to the new South Africa.

One can venture a few general observations, centred on F W. In the next five years he will be cast in three roles in particular: as transitional figure, chief negotiator, and bridge builder.

As a transitional figure he will have to engineer the change from white domination to black participation. The historic role of scaling down the power of the white race rests on his shoulders. In this sense his role is to dismantle more than three centuries of white supremacy. It is an unenviable role, alien to the laws of politics, which are to entrench, enforce and expand power. Reducing power demands great strength, self-denial, and conviction. It means becoming a seed, falling on the earth and dying, so that new life may be born. It means transformation. That is why it is not a role of white surrender, but a role of white conversion to a new role.

As a transitional figure F W does not have an interim role. He will not phase out himself and his government. The concept 'interim government' is misleading. During transition the government broadens its base in the country. It is a transition to integrated government. F W de Klerk and the National Party will continue to play a leading role during the transition as well as afterwards.

As chief negotiator his role is to lead black people into the culture and skills of democratic government, but also to lead whites into a new role in government. It is the historic role of establishing new authority. In this sense F W will become an architect and a designer.

Specifically, he will become the prime negotiator, advocate, watchdog and entrepreneur of white interests. And here he faces many obstacles. In terms of numbers, whites are in a weak negotiating position, the majority euphoria is running high, eager to engulf and minimalize whites, and in the process old antagonisms are being activated on both sides. He has to redefine the role of whites in the face of growing scepticism.

As a bridge builder, F W's role will be to gain the confidence

157

of both black and white. He will have to transform the tradition of mistrust to introduce our population groups to the art of creative political association. The basis of this association is mutual trust, breaking down the stereotypes of each other, and uniting people behind common values and goals. It is the role of a binder, broker, salesman, facilitator, and mediator, who has to conclude a new contract of partnership.

He is ineluctably committed to these three roles. He is like a ship's captain on a stormy sea, because South Africa is still fully in the eye of the storm. It is his task to calm the crew, to give rescue instructions, to read the signals, to plan the strategy, and to steer the ship purposefully towards a hidden harbour surrounded by dangerous reefs. I think he is well equipped for his task, and he has accepted these roles as his calling.

Does F W de Klerk have a credo for the future?

He is not a man for credos in the sense of being caught up in dogmatic politics. He is prepared to cope with changes and choices at crossroads. Being oriented to reality, he believes in solving problems through give-and-take rather than forcing through preconceived ideas.

On the other hand he is a man for credos in the sense that he has deep convictions. I asked him to outline his political credo, projected on the future. This book is full of F W's credos. Once again, and as a summary, he puts it as follows:

'I believe I have a task to lead South Africa into a new era of its history, because it definitely is a new era. The old era is past, once and for all. No-one should find that strange, since history teaches us that dynamic renewal is essential for survival.

'I believe the new era will be a process with different phases. When the final product will be delivered, and what it will look like, no-one knows. The first phase is restructuring to lay the foundation for a new political order. If negotiation does not succeed quickly enough we shall certainly have to seriously consider a phased approach.

'I believe the new political order will and must contain the following elements: a democratic constitution, universal suffrage, no domination, equality before an independent judiciary, the

158

protection of minorities and individual rights, freedom of religion, a healthy economy based on proven economic principles and private initiative, and a dynamic programme for better education, health services, housing and social conditions for all.

'I believe whites will continue to play a strong and influential role in the new South Africa. The decisive factor should be neither numbers nor race. The majority of whites are South Africans who have inherited and earned their rights as citizens of the country. We do not have a post-colonial situation in this country. Whites have enormous potential to serve South Africa at all levels and to the benefit of everyone.

'I believe the black and coloured population are similarly motivated by loyal nationalism and love for their fatherland. The large socio-economic backlogs will have to be drastically corrected in the short, medium and long term. The future has to make provision for this. This, too, is a process, but we have to do our utmost to speed it up.

'I believe the future will prove that compromise can be found on differences. Our worlds are not as far apart as some would have us believe.

'I believe economic progress is highly likely, given our natural resources and the facts that our international relations are being normalized and that we can develop a common market in Southern Africa.

'I believe radicalism will remain a strong force in South Africa. Inflated expectations, power struggles, labour unrest, the residual effects of communist ideology and revolutionary strategy will make great demands on the state and its security forces. I am not talking of a rosy and tranquil future, but I believe the broad mainstream of South Africans will gradually build up South Africa into a society that will be worth living and working in.'

On the road ahead, F W de Klerk and the other leaders will be caught up in seven forces that will govern our day-to-day politics, every single month. Only by the year 2000 shall we be able to see how those forces have developed. These are the seven forces: transitional politics, negotiation politics, compromise politics, persuasive politics, internationalized politics, deadline politics, and venture politics.

2

I referred to transitional politics in my discussion of F W de Klerk's role as a transitional figure. I shall now discuss the broad dynamics of the transition in the years ahead.

There will be a political transition from white domination to power-sharing with blacks, to black majority rule; from limited franchise to universal franchise; and from a group parliament to a general representative parliament. Whites will have to make the transition to acceptance of the inevitable black majority rule, and blacks will have to make the transition to shouldering the yoke of political responsibility. They will have to gain the acceptance of whites, and to do so, they will have to make the political transition from a Marxist-socialist umbilical cord and a one-party, African dictatorship ideology to a Western ideology.

This political transition will have to get its impetus from some form of transitional government on the way to the new system. It is a transition to a new political culture and symbols, and it will demand enormous adaptability.

The transition will also take place at other levels of society. Once all segregationist measures have fallen away, racial mixing in residential areas will increase swiftly and dramatically. There will be a transition to increased urbanization with all its by-products of housing shortages, traffic overload, squatting, an over-supply of labour and increased unemployment. In labour matters, the focus will shift to the upgrading of blacks, increased competition, and labour unrest, with demands for affirmative action. The economic transition will be traumatic for many people, with a drop in profits owing to socio-economic injections for black society, changes in standards, and a shift towards a so-called mixed economy. Education will have to make major adjustments, from segregated schools to integrated schools or private schools that will cost parents a lot of money. The public

160

service and security services will have to adopt an open policy to admit non-whites in large numbers.

I have mentioned only a few basic changes (one could draw up endless catalogues), to illustrate that South Africa will be a society in transition for the next five years and that F W will have to be one of the prime managers of that transition.

Transition has specific characteristics with political consequences. It leads to instability, which could trigger off increased conflict and violence. Since transition goes hand in hand with doubt, people, leaders and policies become hesitant, which is why they tend to advance and retreat during transition. Moreover, the uncertainty and unpredictability of the outcome gives rise to anxiety. Expectations tend to be either too optimistic or too pessimistic. In this regard, Namibia is our laboratory: if they can make the transition successfully, it will have a positive influence on our own transition; if they fail, it will seriously delay and hamper our progress.

Transition also affects the economy, in which uncertainty makes foreign investors hold back and businessmen play a waiting game.

Business leaders – not excepting those in South Africa – are often so focused on short-term profit that it is difficult to induce them to make enormous investments in socio-economic reform.

Transitional politics looms large on F W de Klerk's agenda. If it is not managed effectively it will rebound into chaos. And it requires more than run-of-the-mill management: it is a form of crisis management that calls for quick and daring decisions.

Although transition is bound to have a disruptive effect, there are encouraging signs that the whites – who will have to make the biggest adjustment – are preparing themselves for it.

Alexis de Tocqueville puts it very well:

It is not always when things are going from bad to worse that revolutions break out. On the contrary, it happens more often that when people who have put up with an oppressive rule over a long period without protest suddenly find the government relaxing its pressure, they take up arms against it. Thus the social order overthrown by a revolution is almost always better than the one immediately preceding it, and experience teaches us that, generally speaking, the

161

most perilous moment for a bad government is one when it seeks to mend its ways. Patiently endured so long as it seemed beyond redress, a grievance comes to appear intolerable once the possibility of removing it crosses men's minds.

3

Negotiation politics will be the dominant and overarching dynamics for the next five years.

Hardly anyone would dispute that negotiation is the only way to achieve solutions for South Africa. Negotiation is the chosen option of the South African government, the ANC, the majority of whites, other prominent political players in South Africa, the governments of Southern Africa, and the world community, be it the USSR, the USA or Europe.

Although it is the imperative and obvious choice, it is not a simple one. Negotiation is complex in any situation, and exceptionally so in South Africa. All parties will have to appreciate this, because it will contribute both to more realistic expectations and to a stronger will to make negotiation succeed.

Negotiation or political communication is usually under pressure from conflict, rivalry, urgency, and timing. This pressure will be strong on the road ahead.

In any society, divergent factions, parties, ideals, goals and views are in direct, open and organized confrontation. The pressure of conflict is aggressive and not always bent on seeking solutions; its aim is polarization and the dynamics of tension.

Further pressure is caused by rivalry. The multiplicity of parties and policies in a democracy implies a bid for support in the market place. Through rivalry they are caught up in the dynamics of fierce propaganda for their own views whilst running down those of their opponents. Public criticism of one another is so aggressive that it causes confusion in society.

Add to this the element of urgency. Politics demands action. In times of crisis there is a demand for progress and results. Haste adds a feverish mood to political communication, inflaming expectations, demands, impatience and other emotions to irrational levels.

Timing also plays an important part. The right move at the wrong time or the wrong move at a given time can have disastrous consequences. The political climate of the times has to be taken into account. There are cycles in politics: periods of activism and change are often followed by times of consolidation. Episodes and moments succeed each other. It is like a drama, in which the curtain rises and the act has to be produced.

Negotiation in South Africa is under pressure from these four situations: conflict, rivalry, urgency and timing – and this makes negotiation problematic.

The various components of our society are ranged in conflict. There is strong rivalry for the black vote between radical and more moderate black groups and rivalry for the white vote between the National Party (with its partner the Democratic Party) and the Conservative Party family. There is general rivalry for the black vote among all the parties. The urgency lies in the fact that a long-drawn process of negotiation could have dangerous consequences for South Africa, such as a heightened revolutionary climate and continued isolation from the world community, which could seriously damage our economy. Timing is complicated by the fact that significant numbers of whites and blacks are not ready for the radical shifts that will have to take place in our politics.

A glance at the lines of tension running through our society reveals the following profile:

There is the tension of race. It is a universal fact that racial distinctions cause tension. In South Africa racial differences have additional dimensions of conflict, such as the historic tensions of the early colonial history; the apartheid policy built on racial discrimination; the economic division of haves and have nots that runs mostly along racial lines; and the inequality of numbers, which increases the black majority's sense of injustice and the white minority's feeling of being under threat. As a result, suspicion, vengefulness and anger are prominent in the racial line of tension.

Then there is the tension of culture. South Africa has cultural components of the first, second and third world, and there has been very little acculturation. The cultures of the different groups and a growing cosmopolitian culture are in sharp contrast, as are rural and urban cultures, white and non-white cultures and Afrikaans and English cultures. Ethnic culture draws lines in South Africa. Ours is not an ordinary pluralism; it is a conflict pluralism.

Finally, there is the tension of ideology. Confrontation exists between apartheid (and neo-apartheid) and integration, group government and majority rule, revolution and evolution, socialism and capitalism, and dictatorship and democracy. It runs along the line of tension between the radical and the moderate.

These three lines of tension (race, culture, ideology) are evident at all levels of society: they manifest themselves in divergent views on religion ('black' theology and 'white' theology), on law (indigenous law and Roman-Dutch law), business management and trade unions (politicized black trade unions), and on political organization (struggle politics versus system politics). Tension is also manifested in different nationalities and multi-lingualism.

Against the background of the pressures of conflict, rivalry, urgency and timing as well as the lines of tension of race, culture and ideology, political negotiation in South Africa is particularly complex. Amongst so much conflict, the De Klerk government and leaders such as Mandela and Buthelezi will have no easy task trying to build bridges.

4

The literature on political negotiation identifies specific preconditions for a climate for negotiation. Without that climate, negotiation becomes so much more difficult. Here are some of the prerequisites:

There must be mutual positive expectations about negotiation. The leaders of the different parties and the population in general must have faith in the mutual intention to achieve a settlement.

In South Africa that basic faith must be even stronger. Negative expectations and mutual distrust are definite obstacles. It is openly propagated that blacks want to abuse negotiation to achieve domination, and that whites want to exploit it to divide blacks and institute neo-apartheid with the ostensible consent of blacks. This mistrust means that much spadework remains to be done. One method is to build up a network of negotiation forums at different levels to increase mutual trust. Fortunately, such forums have been springing up like toadstools all over the country. Think-tanks, symposiums, discussion groups and conferences are active everywhere, with blacks and whites conferring on what divides and what binds them. Negotiation cannot take place only at top level; it has to be supported 'from the ground'.

There should be a clearcut decision in favour of settlement through negotiation. There has been considerable progress with this prerequisite. The choice in favour of the armed struggle and a take-over of power through revolution has been buried. But many reservations remain. Elements in the Pan Africanist Congress and other radical black movements are actively encouraging blacks to shoot down negotiation. Right-wing white organizations are trying to muster the white public against negotiation.

The negotiating parties should have more or less evenly balanced power-bases, because negotiation is about weighing up power and reciprocal power pressure to give and to take. The government, fortunately, restored the balance of power when it unbanned the proscribed organizations. Had it not done so, negotiation would have been impossible.

Against the ruling power of the government, which controls an established infrastructure, Parliament and the Defence Force, the ANC can muster the power of an overwhelming majority in numbers. This gives them a veto, a say in negotiations, and the power to block government decisions. Besides, their boycotting and consumer power is growing steadily. This balance of power, as a prerequisite for negotiation, is growing firmer.

165

The parties to negotiation must be legitimate. They must have a mandate for negotiation and for the content of negotiations. They must be recognized representatives, taking part under instructions from their 'constituencies'.

This prerequisite has not been met fully. The black population has only just been organized into political parties, and their self-professed leaders are for the most part not elected leaders; the will of their 'constituencies' has not been tested; no specific mandate has been formulated; and the documents being distributed do not have the official status of a mandate.

This fact is delaying negotiation. As political organization among the black population improves, the agendas will gain legitimacy. Hopefully the accent will then shift from negotiation between white and black to negotiation between political parties, from seeking a racial settlement to seeking settlement between different political agendas.

Much development will have to take place before this requirement is met. The parties to negotiation have to be schooled in the dynamics of negotiation. Good negotiators must have the necessary expertise and attitudes to cope with the give and take of negotiation. They have to be versed in co-operation, flexibility, self-confidence, democratization, empathy, and forming relationships.

The question is whether the actors identified for negotiation in South Africa have the necessary skills. Our political style is still too unyielding, with too much ideology and too little pragmatism; too much paternalism and too little equal association; too much dogmatism, because each is set on having his own plan A accepted with only a few changes, instead of pursuing the compromise solution of a joint plan C. There is too little mutual familiarity with the style, culture and procedures of the opposing parties. South Africa has no tradition of negotiation, its tradition is one of prescription and confrontation, of thesis and antithesis, of all or nothing.

This prerequisite will demand a great deal of work. Fortunately, there are personalities in government and in the ANC who are capable of establishing a true culture of negotiation.

166

The political ecology in the country must stimulate negotiation. Negotiation should not be hampered by disruptive forces; the whole political ecology must be 'open'.

The political ecology has improved tremendously since F W de Klerk came to power. Among the measures that have had a positive effect are the restoration of the right to peaceful protest; the release of political prisoners; the unbanning of political organizations; the lifting of the state of emergency; reducing the influence of the securocrats on the processes of government; the opening of facilities and various further steps to phase out discrimination; the easing of measures surrounding the death penalty, which may now be imposed only by the Appeal Court, and in exceptional circumstances; the appointment of a commission of inquiry into police death squads; the commissioning of a bill of rights; the commissioning of an investigation into constitutional models; amnesty for exiles to return to South Africa without prosecution; the opening of schools to all races, with provision for parental choice; the allocation of billions of rands to alleviate the economic backlog among black people, as a first step towards large-scale efforts to promote economic equality.

The government's positive approach to the independence of Namibia and the attitude of the many African leaders who have held talks with State President De Klerk have caused further shifts in the political ecology, as did his overseas visits and the favourable reaction of the governments in the USA and Europe. Add to this the decline of communism and socialism in Eastern Europe.

Among the factors still hampering the political ecology, the violence and the remaining apartheid laws are the most important. All indications are that these obstacles, too, will be removed in time.

In terms of pre-negotiation requirements, South Africa's prospects have improved considerably. Fair weather is forecast, but much debris of past political storms still has to be cleared up. More positive expectations need to be built up, the open choice in favour of negotiation should be articulated more urgently, the credibility and mandate of black leaders have to be cleared up, and a stronger culture of negotiation has to be established. Too many disturbances in the political climate still point to delays in negotiation.

In negotiations there are usually two or more parties who differ on various issues and whose interests demand that they settle the differences to the benefit of all parties through joint decision-making on differences and agreements, and with the aim of drawing up a 'contract' of compromise.

Settlement communication, therefore, entails removing conflict through compromise. If this is the crux of political negotiation, we can draw the following conclusions:

Conflict is built into negotiation. If it gets the upper hand time and again, it could bring negotiation to a stalemate that might derail negotiations. We should be prepared for the fact that negotiation proceeds in fits and starts. We need nerves of steel and should not give up when there is a hitch. Successful negotiation demands perseverance.

Negotiation is a process. Any process has its own course and should not be forced. Relationships have to develop, and methods, strategies and tactics have to be devised. Finding consensus is a gradual dynamic of persuasion. Old positions have to be relaxed and new ones confirmed.

Negotiation must be structured. Negotiators should know where they are headed and how to get there. They have to be able to make step-by-step decisions in the direction of a compromise that is mutually satisfactory and mutually acceptable. The elements of a game are typical of negotiation: step-by-step gambits; not everything placed on the table at once; hidden motives; demands and rewards; demonstrations, in which the parties play to the grandstand; long pauses after action to allow reaction; and moments of victory and of defeat for each party.

The dynamics of negotiation predicate a lengthy process, and that perseverance will be needed to persist and start from scratch time and again. That negotiation is a process has been made clear so far; now the process itself has to be traced.

I have divided the process into four phases, each with its subphases: exploratory talks, pre-negotiation, negotiation and im-

168

plementation. These phases can be distinguished but not separated. They overlap; sometimes a phase will revert to previous ones or anticipate the next. Negotiation is never an orderly process; it is an open process with many possibilities.

Exploratory talks are characterized by *ad hoc* liaison with different interest groups to test and improve the climate for negotiation. This is the point South Africa had reached by mid-1990.

In the 1989 election the National Party's own power-base gave it a mandate for negotiation. Liaison with various groups followed, including church, business and cultural leaders, leaders of self-governing territories, municipal leaders, and parties in the Tricameral Parliament.

The ANC and its affiliates were invited to negotiate, which set in motion a process of liaison in their own ranks to clear up their position on negotiation in their power-base.

At the time of writing this book, the pre-negotiation phase was in full swing. Hopefully it will have been completed by the time this book is read.

This phase is characterized by arrangements for the official negotiation. Obstacles are removed, methods of negotiation are discussed, and decisions are taken on agendas, participants and procedures. Feed-back is given to the various power-bases, and in the announcement that negotiation will take place, the broad framework of goals, procedures and agendas is made known, as are the place, time and composition of the first full-fledged forum.

Once this process has been completed, the first die has been cast. South Africa, one hopes, will achieve this by the middle of 1991; it could be earlier or later. Since all indications are that these issues are being addressed in the first exploratory phase, I am hopeful that it will be successfully completed sooner rather than later.

Five separate sub-phases will have to be worked through during the official negotiations:

First, the formal phase, in which the structure, agenda, procedures and participants will be settled officially.

Then comes the pioneering phase, characterized by reciprocal statements of intent. Information is given on the stand of each party, its preferences, priorities and 'bottom lines'. Each side attempts to interpret the other and to identify the other's expectations, fears, possible similarities and differences. The parties devise negotiating strategies, develop trust and empathy, and begin to form unofficial alliances. The deliberations develop a unique style.

This is followed by the accommodation phase, which is characterized by overcoming secondary differences and formulating agreements on areas where consensus is readily achieved. Rapport begins to emerge. Mutual problems, fears and reservations are recognized and there is a mutual endeavour to accommodate the demands of the other party. It becomes joint involvement. This phase usually produces a comprehensive statement of intent and the tabulation of general consensus and differences. These are made public after feed-back to the power-bases.

Once this phase is completed, the second die has been cast.

Then comes the toughest phase, final negotiation. Negotiation now focuses on the crucial differences and ultimate priorities. The dynamics are conflict, confrontation and persuasion. This leads to the compromise phase, which produces breakthroughs to give-and-take solutions and in which the middle-ground of Plan B is staked out as a compromise version of the original Plans A and C.

This, in turn, leads to consensus resolutions, the conclusion of binding 'contracts', and the definition of procedures and time-scales for implementing the compromises.

The final die has now been more or less cast.

It is clear that this phase of negotiation is a lengthy one, with many obstacles. Delays and retreats are possible, and so are lengthy stalemates. No-one should be surprised if this phase lasts two years. That would bring the process to 1993.

Then comes the implementation phase. Consensus decisions are implemented according to a schedule after the whole 'contract' has been put to the voters in an election or referendum.

This in itself is a new and lengthy process of phasing out

170

certain things and phasing in new ones. After the referendum in 1994 it could take five years, which would bring us to 1999.

Not that implementation will have to wait until the final product is ready: interim implementation will be needed, for example a mixed cabinet and schemes to make up the blacks' economic backlog.

Everything could happen faster or take longer, depending on delays and success as well as domestic and international situations. The key message to all parties and to the world community, however, should be that negotiation is an evolutionary process, not a revolutionary one. As long as the process continues the hope remains that it will be completed.

F W de Klerk is very realistic about the road of negotiation. His attitude is that it should be shorter rather than longer, because a lengthy process delays stability and foreign investment. But if too many snags cropped up, he would adopt a phased approach. Certain measures, even preliminary decisions, should be implemented, to give proof of progress.

5

The third force in the politics of the next few years is compromise politics.

The essence of negotiation is to find a compromise by way of consensus decisions. The question is whether compromise is possible in South African politics. There is considerable pessimism among both blacks and whites that the divergence of political views will lead to insurmountable polarization and confrontation. This is the dead-end scenario, which the pessimists believe can be resolved only by either a state of permanent revolution and its concomitant oppression and power, or by the escape hatch of partition or territorial division.

As I said earlier in this book, I want to make it clear that the option of partition as an ultimate solution is not necessarily farfetched. It would also, however, have to be a negotiated solution, with general concurrence among black and white and from the international community. Numbers would have to be taken into account in the allocation of land, which would necessarily mean that whites would own far less than they do now.

There could be no 'Boerestaat', rather a division of the country into a northern and southern state. Population groups could hardly be relocated. Full civic rights would have to be granted to all groups in each of the two states. The states could differ in their political and economic systems. No white-dominated state, unless it was a province in a federation, would be tolerable.

The most fruitful way is to seek the alternative compromise of power-sharing in an undivided South Africa. Such a compromise is highly probable, since the opposing parties have often expressed their willingness to accept it. Any form of neo-apartheid, however, would be an unacceptable compromise.

Compromise is further supported by the following factors:

The decline of communism and socialism in Eastern Europe pulled the rug from under the ANC and demonstrated to the government that authoritarian regimes are overthrown by mass uprisings.

The pressure from the East, the West and Africa on the ANC and the South African government to reach a compromise should not be underestimated. Our subcontinent has reached an era of peace initiatives.

The economic realities of South Africa are forcing all groups to find political solutions.

A factor that militates against compromise is that our politics is still too caught up in ideology – we are not yet realistic and pragmatic enough. The negotiation process, however, provides exposure to opposing views, which promotes pragmatism.

Here are some of the important areas in which compromise will have to be found:

A crucial issue is the compromise on group rights or minority rights. One likely compromise is that the government could relinquish the racial divisions in the constitution by repealing the Population Registration Act and replacing it with a policy of freedom of association. Groups (mostly racial groups at this stage) would then share power according to a negotiated formula. The National Party is becoming less set on the idea of a group federation, which would not be a racial federation in name, but would amount to just that. Such a suggestion would in any case require a major compromise from the ANC and its affiliates. I doubt that they would accept it. The National Party itself is beginning to have its doubts, since the whole issue of group rights is being fiercely debated in the inner circles. This debate in Afrikaner circles suggests a willingness to compromise.

The other possibility for compromise is a form of dualism as a transitional measure. It would amount to two parliaments, one white and one black, which would govern jointly in a type of federation based on general affairs and 'own' affairs. Should this compromise be accepted, as an interim measure for a fixed period of ten years, white fears would be allayed, but I doubt whether this would be acceptable either.

The typical solution of the democratic system would be the following compromise: minority rights are linked to political parties and not to other groups such as racial groups; these minorities (organized into political parties) are then protected by proportional representation, which means that minorities are represented at all levels of government according to their support in elections; the right of veto is introduced for minorities at all levels of government, but the issues to be vetoed should not be trivial – they should be laid down in the constitution; an Upper House which specifically represents minorities and has the right to veto specific issues affecting the minority groups. Cultural minorities (such as ethnic groups and language groups) are protected by a Bill of Individual Human Rights and by a clause in the constitution that specifically protects culture, language, own education, community life and religion. This type of compromise has viable possibilities.

Another thorny issue is the compromise on the economic system.

In South Africa the confrontation lies between the capitalist free market system and Marxist socialism. Despite the failure of socialism in Eastern Europe and in Africa, the majority of blacks are in favour of a socialist system.

I think compromise is possible here. The ANC talks of a mixed economy. The principle is that free market mechanisms would remain, but there would be a restructuring under state control to promote large-scale black upliftment and to establish state mechanisms to guard against the exploitation of black people. Different models have been proposed; here is one:

'Wider employee share-ownership schemes; intense training and development of black managers and workers; social responsibility programmes focused on education, housing and infrastructure; broader links between big business and small business. Democratic capitalism or social democracy – a market-orientated system where government has a strong responsibility towards society and intervenes on behalf of the poor and non-educated. Democratic socialism – a system used in Scandinavian countries where the key industries are state-run and the country has a large welfare service. There is large-scale state intervention in the economy on behalf of the poor and some private enterprise and private property and ownership.' (Source unknown.)

A new economic system will require tough negotiation by all parties if a compromise is to be reached.

At the beginning of October 1990 the ANC released a working document on economic policy. The newspapers were flooded with comments, amongst which the following article by Dr Azar P Jammina (*Sunday Star*, October 7, 1990) is an outstanding summary of the economic debate relevant to negotiations.

One of the most promising developments on the South African political and economic scene over the past nine months has been the sudden flowering of the economic debate about what a post-apartheid economy should look like.

However, since it first really took off after the release of Nelson Mandela in February, the debate has been arguably embroiled in far too much rhetoric regarding the merits of nationalisation as opposed to a free-market system.

In such an environment it is all too easy for businessmen, indoctrinated in the notion of so-called free-market economies – even though in many respects the South African economy is far from competitive – to dismiss arrogantly the

'Discussion Document on Economic Policy' published by the ANC as unworkable, before first examining it in detail.

The document is not without its flaws and there are certain glaring analytical omissions and questionable conclusions which need to be addressed in the future economic debate.

But for the first time one has, available for scrutiny, a comprehensive document outlining the ANC's economic thinking, which enables one to recognise that beneath much of the understandable verbiage relating to the need to redress past injustices, the organisation's thinking on economic matters and its economic policy objectives in fact have much in common with those being developed by the present-day government.

The desire to reduce inequality, to make the South African economy less import intensive, effectively to pursue a process of inward industrialisation, to make South Africa less reliant on mineral exports and more industrially oriented, to promote beneficiation, to develop education and skills where they are most needed, to increase the role of local government, to promote the environment – these are all along the same lines of thought as those currently on the Government's economic agenda.

Moreover, the document is conspicuously vague and lacking in specific recommendations as to the means by which the ANC intends attaining its economic objectives, thereby leaving the door wide open for future economic debate.

Taken in conjunction with the proposals set out by the South African Chamber of Business (Sacob) a fortnight ago, which reflected several of the same economic objectives as those contained in the ANC document, one can now verily acknowledge that the real economic debate about what the post-apartheid South African economy should look like has begun.

This is a source of great encouragement, the more so because one senses as never before that the economic objectives of all parties in the debate have so much in common that there is a real chance of achieving consensus on a national economic strategy which is appropriate for a post-apartheid society and which can succeed.

Few would disagree with the ANC's exposition of the massive degree of deprivation of much of the country's population and the organisation's objectives of trying to create jobs; raise real incomes; increase productivity; correct past racial imbalances; feed the people; address the pressing needs of the population in housing, education, health and welfare; provide infrastructure to deprived areas; promote democratic participation in economic life and greater equity in economic ownership; guarantee efficient administration in economic affairs; maintain financial discipline; and so on.

The nub of the problem relates to how to go about achieving these objectives, financially or otherwise, and this is where gaping holes are to be found in its document.

It emphasises a desire to achieve growth and implicitly the objectives outlined above, through redistribution. This can be taken to reflect any of a multitude of possibilities.

Nationalisation is not even mentioned explicitly. Besides the vague terminology of redistribution, however, one can identify only three specific recommendations as to how upliftment should be financed.

Firstly, there is the suggestion that the elimination of bureaucracy and duplication of functions in the civil service within the ambit of the present constitution could result in significant savings.

One cannot agree more as this strikes at the heart of the economy's long-term decline.

By raising government expenditure, the increased cost of bureaucracy implicit in apartheid structures forced taxes up, leaving people with less disposable income, thereby depressing economic growth. At the same time it forced people to save less and borrow more, leading to higher inflation, thereby contributing to the debilitating increase in the concentration of financial power in the hands of a few large organisations to which the ANC justifiably alludes as one of the sources of the extreme concentration of wealth which has harmed economic growth.

What the document fails to recognise, however, is that greater intervention by the State to direct future economic activity, as advocated by the ANC, risks exacerbating the bureaucratic nature of the civil service and raising government expenditure, thereby compounding the dynamics which have been causing the economy's decline.

The failed experience of attempts in many countries to increase State intervention in a non-bureaucratic manner are there for all to see.

The second source of finance for social upliftment suggested by the ANC is the return to a form of prescribed asset requirement whereby financial institutions are obliged to set aside a portion of their cash flows for investment in housing.

This is not unlike the manner in which mortgage finance made available to the South African Housing Trust by financial institutions was able to enjoy prescribed-asset status until last year, when prescribed-asset requirements were abolished.

One cannot disagree with the motives of the ANC in trying to redirect a portion of the massive cash flows in the hands of financial institutions into social upliftment. These institutions have until recently been conspicuous in ignoring their social responsibility towards the masses. They have applied their funds in the pursuit of short-term profit without the vision to recognise that the sacrifice of a portion of short-term profit for social ends could enhance longer-term profitability.

The third source of finance for social upliftment which can be identified in the document is a rise in taxation – specifically on the corporate sector.

This risks killing the goose that lays the golden egg. While we agree with the ANC regarding the need to shift back the burden of tax away from the indi-

176

vidual following the enormous increase in the individual's tax burden over the past decade, the document displays a distinct lack of understanding as to why such changes have taken place.

The document suggests that taxation policy should be used as a means of providing incentives to industrial development, little realising that it has been precisely the exploitation of incentives of this kind which has enabled many corporations to reduce their effective tax-rate.

The document also supports the principle of progressive taxation in which individuals with higher incomes pay proportionately more, without appreciating that it is precisely the interaction of inflation on such a system which has caused the phenomenon of fiscal drag, which has been at the heart of the enormous increase in the tax burden of the individual.

This latter aspect serves to highlight probably the most glaring weakness of the document, namely the manner in which it has skimped over the dynamics of the South African inflation process.

Inflation is responsible for many of the distortions inherent in the current economic structure, such as the lack of savings available for infrastructural and social spending, the paper chase of financial assets on the JSE, the massive concentration of financial and industrial power which is killing entrepreneurship and is itself a source of inflation, and the shift in the burden of tax on to the individual.

Yet inflation is at source the outcome of years of excessive government expenditure.

Until the ANC document, or for that matter any other policy document, can produce a credible plan of action as to how to generate the funding required for social upliftment in a non-inflationary manner, without raising taxation still further in such a way as to annihilate the economy, it can have no real substance.

So long as the temptation is there to address the heightened expectations of the masses instantaneously with no well-considered analysis and time-table for action, inflation and economic decline can be the only outcome.

In this regard Sacob's proposal for a detailed 10-year plan of action to achieve the goals which everyone desires, is constructive and realistic.

Now that the ANC has put its proposals on the table, let the talking begin in earnest to develop consensus for a credible 10-year national economic strategy with specific milestones on the way. In the absence of such a plan, uncertainty will prevail and the economy will continue declining.

Were such a plan to be devised, however, confidence could return and the economic sky could eventually turn out to be very high. The country cannot afford to wait much longer to know where the economy is going.

The State President, too, spelt out the broad terms of his economic policy at the beginning of October 1990. His address

177

to the Natal Chamber of Industry was reported in *Sake-Rapport* on October 7, 1990:

'The aim of government policy is the creation of peace, prosperity, development and participation – a better quality and standard of life in South Africa. This demands constitutional as well as economic reform,' President de Klerk said last week at the annual banquet of the Natal Chamber of Industry.

Economic reform, according to Mr de Klerk, like constitutional reform, is on an irreversible path in South Africa, and is accepted as such by most important countries of the world.

'To solve South Africa's problems a strong and vital economy is necessary, something that was missing for most of the eighties. The low growth rate of the South African economy can be blamed on various factors: two oil crises, serious droughts, a high inflation rate, declining trends in personal savings, the weakening of relationships with reference to the cost of labour in relation to capital, low productivity, a low gold price since the early eighties and an outflow of capital since 1985.'

He referred to his address on February 2 in Parliament, in which he said: 'The Government's basic point of departure is to reduce the role of the public sector in the economy and to give the private sector maximum opportunity for optimal performance.'

During this address President de Klerk summed up the factors that should contribute to the success of the necessary restructuring of the South African economy: the lowering of the inflation rate, personal initiative and saving, strict financial standards and discipline, reform of the tax system and furthering of industrialization.

According to him, the restructuring programme makes provision for the involvement of all South Africans in the market economy and the advancement of entrepreneurship through the encouragement of the informal and small business sectors, the opportunity for each individual to realize his potential, and the necessary education and training to create prosperity.

Individual factors in the programme stressed by President de Klerk are the following: emphasis on all instruments capable of heightening the availability of entrepreneurship, trained labour and capital, the calculated reduction of state spending on defence, but provision for extra spending on the maintenance of law and order, the taking of all possible steps to reduce state spending in real terms during the next three years, the limitation of price and wage increases, and the aim for higher productivity as the responsibility of each individual and institution in the private sector. In addition to measures such as deregulation, commercialization and the advancement of effective competition, certain aspects of economic policy will be revised, such as tax subsidies, regional development and defence.

Then there is the compromise on democracy and the form of

government. The concept of a non-racial democracy, with the protection of minorities, is very vague at this stage. The accent of the compromise would probably fall on central government control. The compromise would lie in decentralization to regional and local authorities.

It would probably be impossible to sell the idea of a federation to blacks, but neither would the typical Westminster state be acceptable to whites. A compromise is clearly called for.

6

The fourth force in the politics of the future is persuasion politics. Whites will have to be persuaded that black majorities are inevitable; blacks will have to be persuaded to respect white fears and aspirations and to move into an equal partnership. Blacks and whites will have to be persuaded to accommodate each other's aspirations.

The question is whether this is attainable, and which methods should be used to achieve it.

It obviously requires an enormous amount of persuasion. Earlier in this book I referred to white fears and unrealistic black expectations. On the side of the whites, the Conservative Party is inflaming these fears, but even in non-Conservative Party circles (more than 60 per cent of whites) there are strong reservations. The business community tends to be uncompromising on the design of the economic system. Public servants feel their job security threatened. Many members of the security forces are finding the new political culture difficult to accept. Within the National Party there is a significant core of cautious and hesitant supporters. Church leaders tell of a wall of reluctance among their members to accept the new dispensation.

In black society the ignorance, utopian expectations, radicalism and impatience for an improved lot are disturbing. In these circles there are power struggles, faction-forming and large-scale political impulsiveness. Equally disturbing is the extremism of the youth and the apparent inability of the leaders to establish a hold over their followers.

It is clear that an extensive re-education process is needed for both white and non-white. This requires time and money, and both are in short supply. Political parties would have to obtain enormous amounts from the private sector to meet this need for intensive information. And the results of this re-education process would be tested as early as 1994, possibly in a referendum.

Fortunately, persuasion politics is a high priority for the National Party, the ANC and Inkatha. F W de Klerk, as a superb persuader, propagandist and informer, provides hope, and so do certain black politicians. Persuasion depends on success upon success, achieved step by step, but also on professional assistance from expert marketers. Money and insight should be devoted to setting up a team of experts to design a persuasion strategy.

Political parties have a variety of activities planned for next year, including think-tanks in constituencies, activating local cells or branches of the parties, advertising campaigns, and mass meetings.

I think the road ahead will bring an increased focus on the most important link in persuasion – the opinion leaders operating in all interest groups. Re-education takes place by converting the opinion leader to the cause, after which his circle of influence is persuaded through the trickle-down effect. Politicians will focus on these opinion leaders, but if the re-education process is to succeed it cannot come from the politicians alone. Each organization, industry or institution will have to practise persuasion down the line of hierarchy, on the pyramid system.

In this regard, three institutions have particular potential as persuaders: churches, the business sector and the media. Churches will have to show greater conviction in bringing the Gospel to bear on conciliation and renewal. I am not suggesting that churches should be misused by turning them into a lobby for politics. In terms of their own mission, churches are involved in settlement politics. F W provides excellent leadership in this regard, too, by regularly conferring with the leaders of the various denominations.

In an interview on this topic he told me: 'It is a matter of principle to me that the church should convey the Biblical guidelines on politics. The vast majority of South Africans are Christians, and churches cannot escape their responsibility to motivate their members to strive for the principles of justice, fairness and communality in politics. Even the non-Christian religious groups in our country have an ethic of neighbourly love and justice, which they should apply to politics. We need the grace of God to persuade people to make a new start, accommodate one another, abandon fears, set aside feuds, and work together for peace and a future in which justice shall be our lodestone. I am not asking for National Party rhetoric from the churches; what I am asking is the message of forgiveness and renewal, also in politics. The churches have a key role to play.'

The business sector is also well placed to play a persuasive role in the community. They have the millions of black workers eating out of their hand, in a manner of speaking. With social responsibility programmes, training, bargaining, the removal of inequalities and the creation of job opportunities and promotion, they can give people confidence in the future.

The media, too have an decisive role in the process of persuasion. Both the mainstream newspapers and the so-called alternative press bolster the politics of the new South Africa with left- and right-wing criticism and reservations. The press will therefore do its share. The ANC will probably try to muster an established newspaper behind it, since it would be difficult to find the money for a new newspaper. It is well known that the influence of newspapers in changing political views is overrated, but I do believe newspapers could shift public opinion in the medium term. As far as the newspapers go, the light is definitely green for persuasion politics.

The battle over the South African Broadcasting Corporation will certainly heat up in the future, since it is the most powerful instrument of persuasion. If it can manage to give all the lead players in politics an equal voice and to plan its strategy so as to give priority to political re-education, history might yet show that the contribution of the electronic media was decisive.

Persuasion politics is the headache of the architects of the new dispensation. F W de Klerk is convinced, however, that the product he and others are trying to sell is a good one, and that South Africa will be ready to cast an overwhelming Yes ballot in three years' time.

7

The other three forces that will determine the future are internationalized politics, deadline politics, and venture politics.

Since South African political development depends heavily on foreign involvement, we can only hope that our present international crises will be defused soon.

Our crises in international terms, as already mentioned, are those of morality, legitimacy, credibility, security, interference, isolation, sanctions and boycotts.

We do not expect miracles within a few months, but it is vital that the international community undertake to do the following within the next year: lift sanctions; provide capital investment and loans; invest in black education, training and housing; and hold extensive interstate discussions on a type of Marshall plan for development.

The business sector will no doubt continue to be very cautious. Eastern Europe is probably a better investment. But foreign governments, in co-operation with their respective private sectors and with the South African government, will have to show enormous initiative to pump astronomical amounts into backing up our new politics with a new economy. If they did so, the negotiation process would benefit, notably in terms of a compromise on economic policy.

Deadline politics means that South Africa has to force through its development within a very short period. Since we have little time, the gradual evolutionary process is too slow for us. Domestic and international observers have given us two years. We shall have to take further leaps, which implies enormous demands on F W de Klerk's leadership. As State President he will constantly have to initiate these advances.

Things could go wrong, for venture politics, too, is an element of the future. The lights could turn either green or red.

In terms of my traffic signal image, the lights turned red for South Africa under P W Botha. The changes introduced by F W de Klerk made the lights turn to amber for South Africa. And that is all we have now: amber lights. Hopefully the lights will turn green in the next year; they could switch back to red.

If the high expectations for our politics fall flat, the anger un-leashed in our contry could spark off renewed uprisings and rev-olution. The rate of reform could be too slow, and it could lose momentum. It could happen that no compromises can be found, that negotiation could bog down in too many stalemates. Our socio-economic situation could deteriorate sharply, which would bring an equal decline in political development.

The seven forces in our politics (transition, negotiation, com-promise, persuasion, international relations, deadlines and risks) could go the way of success or failure. We will be in a state of uncertainty for at least another year.

The government's political attitudes are good. They are open to the future, sincere in their quest for a post-apartheid dispen-sation, aware of the urgency of our situation, prepared to reach major compromises, intent on opening the doors for the nor-malization of our foreign and domestic relations; their style is that of careful planning, their strategy is professional.

They are maintaining the balance between renewal and change, on the one hand, and order and discipline, authority and stability, on the other. They have seen the light as regards the fact that the economy is crucial to success in politics: economic energy is the key to the creation of a new South Af-rica.

The steps taken so far to normalize South Africa are by no means cosmetic.

8

F W de Klerk is at the beginning of his career as South Africa's political leader. For a politician, he is still young (54 years old);

his active career could – by the law of averages – last another 10 years or longer. Even in a black regime it is not inconceivable that he could be State President; that would depend on his continued initiatives and acceptance by the black community. He is not making sums about the duration of his political career. His attitude is that he would want to retire when he felt he had done his duty. In my opinion he is a man with a clear destiny in politics and will continue to play a key role in the decade to come.

He is equipped with personality, intellect and conviction, and he was virtually raised to face the seven forces that will control our politics. He was finely honed for negotiation, compromise and persuasion. He has the inner calm and strength for risks and deadlines. He is intent upon completing the transition in South Africa. And he enjoys international recognition and the broad confidence of all national groups.

So far, he has convincingly passed the test of the scales with his decisions, public appearances, private political talks, and choice of direction.

Within two years he has brought about a transformation in all South Africa's attitudes and relations. He has become the symbol and pioneer of the final removal of apartheid and the architect of a new democratic dispensation. Thus he has become the good messenger who brought hope and vision. In the process he himself has been transformed through his growth in a political philosophy and strategy aimed directly at a democratic solution; yet he remained himself in his modesty and friendliness.

Through it all, he too knows that his final test is still to come, namely the test of success in what he started: the test of perseverance, achievement and resolution, of producing results by controlling the seven forces of our politics. When I mention results, I am not talking about heaven on earth. F W de Klerk cannot possibly solve all the country's problems. The test will be whether he governs in a way that brings us closer to the solution and further away from the abyss.

If he passes this test, another book could be written about him to tell the full story.

184

F W de Klerk has begun to climb the steep stairs of our country's intricate politics. He has engineered a decisive turning-point and placed us on a road from which there will be no turning back. Under his influence the work of all the pioneers of a new political dispensation has been realized. This man is ready for the burden history has laid upon him. His agenda is demanding: another steep flight of stairs awaits.

Greatness is determined by the scope and achievements of a man's spirit and not by status or position. It is not received as a gift, but earned by the strength of deeds. Events will show whether F W de Klerk's continuing contribution will earn him further greatness.

He has opened a new chapter in the history of South Africa. In the loneliness that responsible choices bring, he has cast the die – at enormous risk.